happy anyway
a flint anthology

EDITED BY SCOTT ATKINSON

First Edition 2016.

Printed in Michigan

ISBN: 978-0-9968367-1-5

Belt Publishing
1667 E. 40th Street #1G1
Cleveland, Ohio 44103
www.beltmag.com

Cover Photo & Book Design by Shane Gramling | www.ShaneGramling.com

Also from
Belt Publishing

The Cleveland Neighborhood Guidebook

How to Live in Detroit Without Being a Jackass

The Pittsburgh Anthology

Car Bombs to Cookie Tables:
The Youngstown Anthology

A Detroit Anthology

The Cincinnati Anthology

Rust Belt Chic: The Cleveland Anthology

Table of Contents

Introduction: Greetings from the Middle   6

Paragraph of Doom   10
GORDON YOUNG

Love and Survival: A Flint Romance   14
LAYLA MEILLIER

Beam, Arch, Pillar, Porch: A Love Story   18
JAN WORTH-NELSON

Fresh to Death   28
ERIC WOODYARD

No Pawnshops for Old Stories   34
TEDDY ROBERTSON

The Spirit of Sam Jones   38
BOB CAMPBELL

Flintlock   46
STEPHANIE CARPENTER

City Beat: Covering Hoops in Basketball City, USA   52
PATRICK HAYES

Flint Out Loud   72
TRACI CURRIE

Feeling a Little Subprime   78
TEDDY ROBERTSON

2302 Welch   84
WILL CRONIN

Being Bama   90
BECKY WILSON

Too Fancy for Flint?   96
ANDREW MORTON

Do You Realize? 104
LAYLA MEILLIER

When Home Says, "Go" 108
SARAH CARSON

Garden Party 118
NIC CUSTER

The Wild West on the Eastside 126
STACIE SCHERMAN

Hyphen Flint 134
JAMES O'DEA

Growing Up Eastside 138
MELISSA RICHARDSON

Meet the Flintstones 146
EDWARD MCCLELLAND

A Boy and His Graveyard: Resurrecting the History
and Mysteries of Glenwood Cemetery 154
SARAH MITCHELL

Dubiously Flint: Remembering (and Forgetting)
My Grandmother's Stories 164
KATIE CURNOW

A People's Park 170
EMMA DAVIS

Bathtime 182
CONNOR COYNE

Contributors 188

Acknowledgements 194

Introduction:
Greetings from
the Middle

I had just started writing about Flint when I found myself sitting next to Michael Moore, listening to him talk about what Flint had to offer the world. There were perhaps eight of us crammed into the small and smoke-stained meeting room of Flint's now-defunct alternative monthly paper, *The Uncommon Sense*. We were on the second floor, above a small T-shirt shop that was, at the time (this was the early 2000s), one of the few businesses you'd find downtown. We'd invited him because he too had once run a small paper in Flint, work that seemed more noble when no one was making money, the editor wore untied work boots, and the highest trained reporter was the new guy who'd just started journalism school. Never mind the arguments we'd had over his films, the things some of us had said, positive we'd never be face to face with Michael Moore. Because here he was, talking about Flint.

He was talking about the Beatles.

The best art, he said, did not come straight from places like New York or London, but rather from the Liverpools and Flints of the world, the places that know what it means to struggle. The places where many people have known nothing but struggle.

We nodded along with a beatnik-like intensity. Yeah, man. Because when you say it like that, it sounds special. It's downright romantic. We don't want to believe that our celebrities and heroes are manufactured or had it easy. We need them to be the result of an honest struggle, proof that you can come out the other side. New Jersey has Sinatra and Springsteen. Detroit? Take your pick: Eminem, Joe Louis, the entirety of Motown. Flint's churned out its own share as well—and what would they be to us without the city that made them? When rapper Jon Connor signed with Dr. Dre, would we have seen him the same way if he hadn't, just months before, been recording and mixing in his mother's basement? When Claressa Shields won the gold medal, was it just her boxing that impressed us, or did we extend her fighting into a metaphor beyond the ring? These stories are about what they've accomplished (and not accomplished) in spite of everything. In spite of Flint.

We wouldn't want it any other way, so long as the struggle is in the past, something we know can be overcome. We want our heroes singing or rapping or telling us with every slam dunk that it has all been done, it's all been gone through. It's our own little bit of proof that our own struggles, too, can be overcome. We want, in other words, happy endings.

You will find no such endings here. That is not to say you will not find happiness, but what you will find are a lot of middles, stories about continued attempts at endings. Stacie Scherman writes about her father, a man protecting what's left of a warehouse that burned down and the retirement that went up in flames along with it, wondering when, or if, his share of the American dream will ever come. Layla Meillier, our youngest contributor, writes with heartbreaking detail about what it means to grow up in Flint, to wonder what is on the other side of the horizon for her and for the city that has done so much to define her.

These are stories from the middle. They are stories of triumph not because anything has been won, but because they are stories of Flint's continued fight. They are stories that remind us you cannot ride into the sunset forever, that life goes on, not always easily.

That might still sound romantic. It is not.

There is a steadfastness people like to mention when talking about the people of Flint. A grittiness. Call it blue-collar if you like. It is a pragmatic mindset, one that is not awaiting some grand arrival, but simply pushing forward. It's a philosophy borne, perhaps, out of knowing that tomorrow you have to get up and do it all over again—and again and again until you die. It's an understanding that life is one big middle. And once you're smart enough to understand that, you realize that even when it's tough you find what happiness you can.

That is where the title of this book comes from. I first used it in a story for *Belt Magazine*, writing about yet another struggle that has been heaped upon Flint: a poisoned water supply. As this collection makes its way to print, Flint is still so deeply into the middle of the crisis it is unclear when, or how, it will end. There still aren't enough answers or solutions, and there's no way to know how this will be remembered in ten or twenty or one hundred years. It was when writing about the water crisis that I found Pastor Bobby, a man who knows the middle better than anyone. He runs a homeless shelter on Flint's north side, only a few blocks from the once-sprawling car factory so big it was called Buick City. He had helped people through all of the problems the city had to offer—crime, joblessness, homelessness, hopelessness. And when the water went bad, he took that on, too.

"He's so happy," I wrote. "In his business, if it can be called a business, you need to be. It's a particular kind of happiness, a Flint happiness, not meaning so much that you're happy, but that you're happy anyway."

Flint happiness is a fought-for happiness, an earned happiness. It's a happiness that carries an asterisk, a never-ending footnote of stories that demand you understand and respect the history of where everything good in the city came from. And continues to.

Those are the stories you will find here.

Happy reading.

Scott Atkinson
Flint, Michigan

Paragraph of Doom

GORDON YOUNG

W *hen you sit down to read a story about Flint, you know it's coming. Somewhere, somehow there must be a synopsis of the city's tragic fall, a compressed version of its four-decade socio-economic swan dive. It's not easy to pull off. Think of condensing* The History of the Decline and Fall of the Roman Empire *down to 750 words or less. The worst end up sounding like they were dictated by a weepy drunk at a class reunion. The best convey the carnage but leave the city and its residents with their dignity intact. I've cobbled together a collection of verbatim descriptions from various writers—some with the talent and empathy to take on Flint, and others not worthy of carrying* Rivethead *author Ben Hamper's pencil case—to create the ultimate Flint Paragraph of Doom. Read it and weep.*

Flint is an incredibly unique place. Historically, it is the American dream turned into the American nightmare.[1] It's the ultimate, American post-industrial ghost town.[2] For decades Flint has been a symbol as much as a place: it's a stand-in for American rust belt decline.[3] This is America's most apocalyptic, violent city.[4] Flint hasn't always been this dangerous or depressing.[5] The Vehicle City was once home to mile-long car plants and a thriving, blue-collar middle class.[6] The birthplace of thud-rockers Grand Funk Railroad, game show geek Bob Eubanks and a hobby

---

1   Canepari, Zackary and Cooper, Drea. "Youngest Female Olympic Boxer Is Subject of New Kickstarter Doc." Interview by P. McCollough. *Wired*, July 31, 2012. http://www.wired.com/2012/07/california-is-a-place-claressa-t-rex-shields/

2   Joe Weisenthal, "America's Most Depressing Places," *Business Insider*, May 14, 2009. http://www.businessinsider.com/worstcities/americas-most-depressing-places-flint-michigan

3   Richard Warnica, "Flint, Michigan: Where the pipes poison the water and even the nice parts of town are dotted with vacant homes," *National Post*, February 1, 2016. http://news.nationalpost.com/news/world/flint-michigan

4   Laura Dimon, "This is One of America's Most Violent Cities—And It Deserves More Attention," *Policy. Mic*, December 26, 2013. http://mic.com/articles/77225/this-is-one-of-america-s-most-violent-cities-and-it-deserves-more-attention#.LstEg0rGz

5   Christina Sterbenz and Erin Fuchs, "How Flint, Michigan Became The Most Dangerous City In America," *Business Insider*, June 16, 2013. http://www.businessinsider.com/why-is-flint-michigan-dangerous-2013-6

6   Warnica, "Flint, Michigan: Where the pipes poison the water and even the nice parts of town are dotted with vacant homes."

shop called General Motors.[7] Today, with its automotive workforce down to 6,000, less than a tenth of its 1970s prime, Flint has the highest homicide rate in the nation and an average home sale price of $15,000.[8] Flint isn't Vehicle City anymore. The Buick City complex is gone. The spark-plug plant is gone. Fisher Body is gone. What Flint is now is one of America's murder capitals.[9] A big part of the problem is there just aren't enough jail cells for all the criminals.[10] If all the empty houses, buildings, and vacant lots were consolidated, there would be ten square miles of blight in the city.[11] Flint has been demolishing homes as the city shrinks with residents leaving in search of jobs.[12] A city built to manufacture cars would be returned in large measure to the forest primeval.[13] Now, for many, the catastrophe of a water supply that may be poisoned indefinitely appears to be the final insult.[14] Apparently, Flint's citizens needed to keep drinking poisoned water for a year before the state could figure out how to unpoison their water.[15] Flint now drowns in the hell that has become of much of America's Rust Belt.[16] It is not, to state the obvious, a fun-loving college town like Ann Arbor.[17] It's a dismal cascade of dreck, but it's still home.[18]

7   Ben Hamper, *Rivethead: Tales from the Assembly Line* (New York: Warner Books, 1991), 15.

8   Edward McClelland, "Here's what your foreign cars have done to Michigan," *Washington Post*, September 28, 2015. https://www.washingtonpost.com/posteverything/wp/2015/09/28/heres-what-your-foreign-cars-have-done-to-michigan/

9   Charlie LeDuff, "Riding Along With the Cops in Murdertown, U.S.A.," *New York Times Magazine*, April 15, 2011. http://www.nytimes.com/2011/04/17/magazine/mag-17YouRhere-t.html?_r=0

10   *Roger & Me*. Dir. Michael Moore. Warner Bros. 1989. (Clip of local newscast.)

11   Gordon Young, *Teardown: Memoir of a Vanishing City* (Berkeley, California: UC Press, 2013), 3.

12   Kurt Badenhausen, "America's Most Miserable Cities, 2013," *Forbes*, February 21, 2013. http://www.forbes.com/pictures/mli45lmhg/2-flint-mich/

13   David Streitfeld, "An Effort to Save Flint, Mich. by Shrinking It," *New York Times*, April 21, 2009. http://www.nytimes.com/2009/04/22/business/22flint.html

14   Lenny Bernstein, "Hope—and clean water—remains elusive for the people of Flint," *Washington Post*, February 7, 2016. https://www.washingtonpost.com/national/health-science/for-the-people-of-flint-hope--and-clean-water--remains-elusive/2016/02/06/1a6013c0-caa0-11e5-88ff-e2d1b4289c2f_story.html

15   Stephen Rodrick, "Who Poisoned Flint, Michigan?" *Rolling Stone*, January 22, 2016.http://www.rollingstone.com/politics/news/who-poisoned-flint-michigan-20160122#ixzz41OTkKFLH

16   Dimon, "This is One of America's Most Violent Cities—And It Deserves More Attention."

17   Gordon Young, "International Students Find the American Dream…in Flint," *New York Times*, October 27, 2015. http://www.nytimes.com/2015/11/01/education/edlife/international-students-find-the-american-dream-in-flint.html?_r=0

18   Ben Hamper, email message to author, June 28, 2009.

GORDON YOUNG

Love and Survival: A Flint Romance

LAYLA MEILLIER

I could not appreciate what Flint had taught me until I let myself fall in love. For years I dodged it; I could not even commit to a favorite color or TV show, let alone a person. When you're not in love you can never be hurt in such a vulnerable way. As a young woman, I don't blame this city for my lack of puppy love; I blame this city for my fear of feeling vulnerable.

My first love was a bike. A sleek hunk of purple pipe with sparkly wheels and handlebars. I collaged my bike in goofy stickers I had begged my mom to buy me at Rite-Aid one day. I was not permitted to leave my neighborhood, but I did not mind because my world seemed vast.

At the time, we lived on Mountain Avenue in the College Cultural neighborhood, a place in the city considered more suburban without a too-safe uniformity. There, homes range in size and era of origin and the people tend to be unique and artsy. They look out for one another. In other words, it's a go-to spot for young couples moving to Flint with extra money. The house we had was a brick duplex that looked like a German cottage. My stepdad owned a glass company in the north end that has long since been closed down. In its day, the company did well. There is never a scarcity of broken glass in Flint.

Although I was told time and time again to put my bike in our doorless garage behind the house each night before bed, one night, like ya do, I forgot. I left the nose of my bike barely peeking out from behind the house. To my naive surprise, someone took it in the night.

The news of this evoked a sadness I was not familiar with at the age of ten. At ten, one cries easily, pouts easily, sobs easily, but I could not make a sound. I felt as though my eyes had turned to stone and I wished I could not see out of them. My parents told me about the theft in an awkward family meeting, standing in our cramped kitchen. They filled me in on the normalcy of this sort of situation in my hometown:

"There is nothing we can do. The police are too busy with other things. This happens all the time."

I went to my bedroom in a haze. A week went by and I didn't even go outside to play; instead, I took to throwing weird shit down our dumbwaiters and retrieving it in the basement laundry hamper. Then, one day, my bike was back!

"They found it," was all I was told by my numbly shocked mother.

Years later, I was hanging out with my now ex-stepdad, catching up around the holidays, and he was feeling a little toasty. "I lied to you that time when we were living on Mountain," he said.

"What?"

"I lied about your bike."

"What do you mean? What happened to my bike?"

"The police never found it."

"Yes they did; it was my bike..."

"Yeah, but I found it. Not the police." I stared at him in shock as he unfolded the tale of how he happened to be driving through the east side one day, looking for a house that needed an estimate pre-installation of new glass, in his big company truck, and he noticed a yard that was "covered in colorful kid shit." He figured he'd check it out. Lo and behold, my bike was amongst the mismatched wreckage. He planned to confront the people living there, a reasonable goal for a man of his size, covered in intimidating tattoos.

"I found your bike, laying on its side, on the ground."

"Those bastards," I said. I never let my bike lay on the ground. I always used a kickstand.

"Yeah, right, the bastards! So I stole the bike back."

"What? In the middle of the day?"

"Yup. I went and knocked on the door but no one came. So I just took it. I slid it in my glass rack and took off."

I needed some time to process this before I asked, "Why didn't you ever tell me?"

"Well, because I never wanted you to think stealing back was the answer and I guess I didn't want you to feel like the police can never help you."

Fair enough. Either way, since that day, I've been paranoid about my stuff. I don't feel so bad about losing things as having them exposed. I would rather my belongings be reasonably lost and safe than displayed. When I was a preteen and spent time walking around the city alone, I wore baggy clothing. I stuffed my hair up in a neutral cap but never put my hood up—with it up I can never see my peripherals—unless I felt terribly angsty that day like I didn't care if someone snuck up behind me. Don't leave your stuff out; don't be a female; don't wear pastels; don't fall in love. It's all too painfully vulnerable. Until one day, years into my aged-cheese adolescence, it hit me, while I was lying in bed with my lover.

He was sleeping and I was not. I watched him for a few minutes, closed his jaw when it popped open and his stank morning breath burned my eyes. I put my face real close up to his and pretended time had stopped in the moment just before a kiss and we were frozen. And then I got that feeling, like before when I should have been crying but I couldn't and my eyeballs turned to stone. I realized he wasn't vulnerable because I did not want to hurt him. I was taking ownership of my vulnerability and forgetting the dependence vulnerability has on external forces. What about trust? If you are trusting, you are vulnerable ... but will external forces feel more inclined to hurt you if you trust them? No. Is life about always putting your bike safely in the garage? No.

I don't typically wear my heart on my sleeve but when others need it, I leave it peeking out from behind the house and let them take it for a week. It's easy to get let down by this city and get angry and look at everyone on the street like they might have to fight you, but that just creates more problems. I'm still here because the lessons are complicated and I want more than anything just to learn how to be a good human being, to be vulnerable, and to love.

Beam, Arch, Pillar, Porch: A Love Story

JAN WORTH-NELSON

hen I came to Flint for a social work job in 1981, I was ready to launch my adult life. Somewhat desperate for it, as I recall.

My adulthood was delayed to start with. I'd fled to the West Coast after an adequate Midwest education, spent five years as a kid reporter in Southern California, slept with a couple of dozen guys—the way we first-Pill, pre-AIDS gals did back then—and generally reveled in my sunny '70s choices. Then I added two years in the Peace Corps—a powerful adventure mostly pursued by the young—and then chalked up two years in Ann Arbor in graduate school, yet another exercise in late adolescence and subjugation to somebody else's supposedly better judgments.

By the time I got to Flint, I was thirty-one, never married, childless. My twenties had been flamboyant, memorable, exhilarating. But then I was thirty-one and I skidded. I remember saying to myself something like, "You're an emotional isolate, kid. When are you going to have somebody to love, etcetera?"

I was ready to grow up somewhere. I just never thought it would be Flint for the next thirty-five years. I thought I would put in a few years, pay off some grad school debts, and then move on. I don't know where I thought I would go. Sometimes I think, how could this have happened? One night recently I heard Rachel Maddow say on TV, parsing our latest misery, "Is Flint, Michigan, still habitable?" and for a moment, I felt like everything was falling apart. My nerves faltered and I wondered how I—how any of us—have managed to be here all this time.

But before this confessional gets too grim, I want to say my story has a lot of happiness in it. You might not even have to wait till the end—I will fast-forward a little of it now. I'm not one to celebrate Horatio Alger-ish life plans. I'm more of a "so it goes" girl, who's had some decent luck along with a real life of missteps, bungled love, and, in certain surprise circumstances, requited yearning. Here's the thing: sometimes when I get up in the morning and look out the window into my back yard, where finches scallop onto the bird feeder and a cardinal flashes red in the paper birch, I feel peace and something I can only describe as joy. So there, you doubters. It can happen. Even in Flint.

And at the heart of it is my house.

My Flint house is crucially interwoven with the life I have made here—a hard-won architecture of endurance, not just the bitter, stoical kind. Rather, this architecture, one that somebody designed before I even moved in, is rich in generosity, hospitality, and spirit. But that's getting ahead of the story.

Somewhere along the line, I found Alain de Botton's book *The Architecture of Happiness.* All the drama and turmoil of my life in Flint, as I reflect on it, is shaped and represented by the shelter I have found: two apartments, three houses, all memorable, all refuges—structures I confess I loved more than people because in a town where so much is broken, my houses were whole, already there to comfort me, habitations I came back to time and again with relief and gratitude.

The houses of Flint—those that remain, those that we have loved partly because they are still beautiful, because we wanted them and could buy them and live in them—those houses are one of the gifts of this tumultuous town and the part of my life here that has been full of healing grace.

Botton describes how one of his own houses has "grown into a knowledgeable witness," and how, "although this house may lack solutions to a great many of its occupants' ills, its rooms nevertheless give evidence of a happiness to which architecture has made its distinctive contribution." My Flint homes, enduring evidence of someone's attentive eye, a plan that includes loveliness, have helped me transcend the banalities of the city's stumbling politics, the tragedies of its losses and deteriorations. My Flint homes argue for the endurance of good over evil, beauty over ugliness, sanctuary over isolation.

Avon Street

My first place was a cozy, dark-paneled walk-up two blocks from downtown in East Village, a neighborhood of old houses, many built in the late 19th or early 20th centuries, mostly subdivided and down at the heel, with big trees remaining. My place, built in 1870, had slanted ceilings and dormer windows you couldn't do much with facing the street. It had a brick fireplace built up two feet off the floor, and it worked—to me an exotic feature of the second story flat. Eventually I kept little pallets of firewood on the hearth.

The first night I slept there, I sat on the living room floor staring out the wavy, clouded glass, eating junk food because my paltry truckload of grad-school furniture hadn't yet arrived. I had a small boom box. Playing around with it, I was surprised to come upon some jazz. It turned out to be a local public radio station, broadcasting from the basement of the high school three blocks away. The station is long shuttered and the high school abandoned, but that night in 1981, when I needed it, the music was still there.

The next morning, startled, I woke up to what sounded like a clopping horse. Can't be, I mumbled. I scrambled up to one of the dormer windows and saw that horse, hooked up to a little cart with a young bearded guy at the reins. Eventually I found out the horse, named Ali, was grandfathered in, stabled in a rickety old place across the street. I wrote a serialized children's story about that horse and its owner for the *Flint Journal* one Christmas season, an odd little project for me. In my story, the horse talked and so did a sociable squirrel, as I recall. I don't remember the plot—it had an adequate amount of conflict and everybody ended up happy. Ali's owner John, who was called Cliff the Plumber in my tale, steered his horse in the Christmas parade that year and children went downtown just to see him. Ironic, considering the current crisis, that the hero in my 1980s story was a plumber.

Eventually John had to move Ali out of the stable and then John himself moved to Ann Arbor, where I understand he still is having a happy life.

I was within walking distance of a legendary downtown bar, Hat's Pub, where they had poetry nights. I got up my nerve and joined in after a day of work with an unending stream of clients who were sliding-scale abused and abusers, SSI recipients, alcoholics, depressed laid-off auto workers, schizophrenics. Many smelly. We were payee/guardians for a lot of them. One of my clients fell off a barstool at a strip bar named Lafferty's Titty City across from the old manufacturing complex along the river, endearingly known as Chevy in the Hole. She tried to refuse treatment for a broken leg. I signed the papers. Another, one of my favorites in fact, pooped in my car out of nervousness on his way to be placed in a nursing home. His one wish when he got there was head cheese. I found some and delivered it the next day.

Hat's Pub came down decades ago and, to quote Joni Mitchell, they put up a parking lot. But not before years of Flint poetry happened. That scene was salve for my soul. I had some stuff to try out, a lot of dramatic loneliness and sex—I was reading Anaïs Nin. The joint offered recurring great music, cheap beer, good subs, autoworkers, and students from the University of Michigan-Flint mixing it up night after night. I fell in love with one of the other poets. One icy winter night we slipped and slid from the bar to my beat-up VW Bug, and I drove him to my walkup. He paused just inside the door, the dark paneling a warm cloak around us. Almost crazy with embarrassment, he said he had to tell me something: he had false teeth. Too much Coke when he was a kid, or something, he said. I don't care, I said. Kiss me.

Later he wrote, "In your eyes is that patch of ice I want my wheels to hit."

That was one classic Flint romance.

He was married and it was messy, but he moved into that little walkup and we slept on a mattress on the floor. His twelve-year-old son came to visit and we went across the street and he gave an apple to the horse. The boy's mother filed for divorce and child support was arranged. We were broke all the time but had enough for beer, wine, and books. A scrawny street cat adopted us and had a litter in the living room. We gave away two and kept one. We named him Tater and he lived with us for nineteen years.

Seventh Street

We moved out of the walkup, taking Tater with us. His mother refused to go, escaping back to her Avon Street territory so often we finally left her there, a neighbor taking her in.

Our house, the first one I ever owned, sat on a dead end just outside the elaborate brick gate to one of Flint's anachronistic mansions. We benefitted from the grounds of the estate, thick woods that secured us in a secret corner of the city. The house was a sturdy square stucco, built in 1919. We heard it had been a parsonage, which made me, a preacher's kid, very happy. We stripped out moldy carpet and made the wood floors gleam. We patched and repainted walls and installed a brass railing up the stairs.

It was in Fairfield Village, a section of the city between I-475, I-69, and the more upscale Woodlawn Park. Some of its streets used to extend right into downtown, but now the freeways cut it off, after clear-cut urban renewal took out an old African-American community called Floral Park. I didn't understand that history when we bought the place, but now, more attuned to the city's history of racial segregation and housing discrimination, I understand why sometimes Seventh Street seemed full of ghosts. People had been uprooted within spitting distance; a whole vibrant community had been dislodged.

I married that poet. It's funny, the things you remember. Our wedding, with all the furniture pushed back in the living room and dining room, folding chairs lined up. How my mother pulled out the expensive blue brocade dress she'd worn for my older sister's wedding two decades before, and how she ended up on her knees in that dress, in the back yard, pulling up a bunch of measly carrots I had meant to harvest a week before. How did I let her do that?

My dad, well into failing mental acuity, in full ministerial regalia, black robe, white stole, forgetting my groom's first name. My father silhouetted, craggy like an old prophet, the big picture window behind him. He called him Denny, or Tommy, or Donny—I don't remember for sure. My love and I facing him, blinded by the glare, our crazy histories oscillating behind us.

How somebody got in a fight during the reception and we told them to take it out to the street and they did.

How we found champagne corks in the grass in the back yard for months— years—afterward.

My father noticed the sixteen-inch beams in the basement of that house. "These are substantial, not cheap construction," I remember him saying. It meant a lot to me, suggesting I had chosen wisely, if not in my husband, whom my father never trusted, then in the house we picked.

How every summer we strung twine from the upstairs windows on the back of the house for morning glories, and how the morning glories proliferated, filling the whole back wall of the house: blue trumpets.

How I tried to make some elaborate crêpe dish for a dinner party, and the stack of fancy crêpes collapsed into a puddle of hollandaise at the table in front of the guests and by then I was already drunk, as we often were back then, and as I fluttered over the mess my husband said, "Calm down."

How I stood up on a chair at some dinner party to tell a joke about the case of reverse digestion, and how I still love that half-drunk woman in her thirties raving and laughing, performing in winey ecstasy.

How I couldn't get my drunk husband out of the car by myself after a long night at Rube's, a blues bar up on Chevrolet Avenue, and two other friends helped me and he couldn't get upstairs so we left him on the couch, muttering and enraged.

How we used to roll up the carpet and do the Silly Walk and boogie to James Brown. Sweaty and ardent and flinging our arms up in the air.

How I stood at the kitchen window staring out, then wracked and weeping one day, realizing finally, after two botched pregnancies, and ultimately a final messy miscarriage, I was not going to have a child. My husband coming up behind me and whispering, "We can try again," and me saying, "No, I am done."

And how we went to Barbados instead that year and drank a lot of rum.

His first wife committed suicide. My husband was the only one Hurley Hospital knew to call, and when he went in to see her, he thought she was still alive as he sat there stroking her hand. "No, she's gone," someone finally told him.

"She's dead," he cried when he found me in the waiting room, unbelieving, shocked, and guilty. We kept her funeral dress, a red one, in our closet for a few days because it seemed nobody else knew what to do.

His son, by then eighteen and home from college, desolate, sat at the kitchen table across from me and said, "Why did this happen?" and we didn't know what to say.

Then, I started to grow back into some semblance of my self—a self I'd lost sight of in all my Flint travails. I got an MFA in poetry and some seed of hope, of resurrection, sprouted. We were both publishing; we won grants and traveled around as a couple, doing our literary thing. Here's some of that happiness I promised. We were good together.

But eventually our marriage broke up. I suppose it was fate—two poets, each full of old wounds and guilts and drinking too much and yearning for something we couldn't quite deliver. When we broke up I'd been in Flint for twenty years. What had I done? How could I start over? When I was looking for another place to live I walked back to Avon Street and stood in front of it, disconsolate, lost in a sense that my life had come to nothing.

I was teaching by then. My parents had died and left me just enough money to launch a semblance of a new adulthood. I moved into a high-ceilinged Art Deco apartment downtown. I reconnected with a lover from twenty-five years earlier, and he came to Flint to court me. Again and again.

Eventually my husband put the Seventh Street house up for sale, married another woman, and moved up north.

I have always walked when my soul needs reprieve. After I moved out, after my husband moved out, I used to walk by that house on Seventh Street. Nobody bought it for a long time. I would sit on the front porch, feeling the house's emptiness in my own body. I loved—and still love—the two giant oaks in the front yard that used to bathe our bedroom in gold every fall.

My new/old lover extended his visits: three-day weekends, then a week, then two. My apartment was intimate, often hot. The building's ancient boiler clanked and banged all night, like the noise of my frayed nerves. Sirens from the Fifth Street Fire Station wailed at all hours, as if the whole world was in a state of emergency.

And once again, the sanctuary of houses was part of my redemption. In an act of audacity, both of us clambering out of personal ruins, Ted and I bought a house together—here, in troubled Flint.

That Ted understood how much I needed a house, a shelter of my own that could be the refuge of my heart, is to this day one of the things that binds me to him.

Maxine Street #1

Even now—or especially now—Flint is known as a demolition "rock star," Christina Kelly, a project director of the Genesee County Land Bank, told *East Village Magazine* last December. We are used to things being demolished. The Land Bank recently announced funds enabling close to 3,000 demolitions after hundreds more in the last several years. In general, these are good cleanups—the earth's return to clover and urban gardens a sign of the community's gradual adaptation to its losses.

But what remains matters to us, too. Some of what is left is so beautiful. I return to De Botton: "Although we belong to a species which spends an alarming amount of its time blowing things up," he writes, "every now and then we are moved to add gargoyles or garlands, stars or wreaths, to our buildings for no practical reason whatever. In the finest of these flourishes, we can read signs of goodness in a material register, a form of frozen benevolence.

"We see in the evidence of those sides of human nature which enable us to thrive rather than simply survive…we need a culture confident enough about its pragmatism and aggression that it can also acknowledge the contrary demands of vulnerability and play—a culture, that is, sufficiently unthreatened by weakness and decadence as to allow for visible celebrations of tenderness." In all my years with my first husband I used to jog through Woodlawn Park from Fairfield Village and gape at the bigger, more ostentatious houses, artifacts of Flint's glory days. I'm not a materialist, but I can't explain it: I felt like something had eluded me. Maybe it was that superfluous tenderness—in my vulnerability, "signs of goodness," a visible celebration of a life of hope.

When we moved to Maxine Street, in the College Cultural neighborhood adjoining Woodlawn Park, some old restlessness was finally stilled. I felt as if I'd matured; maybe I was, at last, a woman in full. We got married.

The house wasn't the biggest or most impressive, but it was solid—a square colonial, upright and orderly—four rooms up, four rooms down, its windows providing bright light in every season. The sunniness of that place reflected the light in my life, my gradually healing heart.

It had amazing crown molding, layered and elegant, with no apparent reason except to create a frame of loveliness to look up to. Its arches into the living room and dining room softened the squareishness of the colonial design. It felt good to be in those rooms. I could sit on the west-facing back porch and see the sunset, or meditate in the morning in our east-facing bedroom. I eked out a small herb garden, hauling in boulders from a local stone yard, and put up birdfeeders. Finches, cardinals, and nuthatches found us in abundance. I finished my novel, retired from my teaching job, loved my husband, walked with my neighbors. We built on a new front porch, with two modest columns topped by Ionic capitals — a design touch I remembered from my favorite childhood parsonage. A gifted craftsman put in a new sidewalk, embedded with etched icons: yin-yang, sunburst, honeybee, chambered nautilus. We had a neighborhood party to celebrate, with a hot dog cart in the driveway doling out Flint's favorite coneys. It was a happy day.

Maxine Street #2

We loved our first Maxine Street house, and in fact we still own it, but we also had a crush on the house next door. We got to know our neighbor Mary Helen very well — her two little yippy dogs at the fence, her kitchen where she served us lamb chops and asparagus, with a couple of beers from time to time. The mail carrier said Mary Helen and I were the only ones on the street to get the New Yorker; we gabbed about our favorite stories and bitched about the poetry over her back fence.

After a few years, she had to move to assisted living and a family with five children moved in — a noisy, boisterous bunch. Then, through a series of surprises, they abruptly moved out and the house came up for sale.

In those nerve-wracking months when we didn't know what would happen, Mary Helen's daughter, who was managing the land contract, gave me a key. Day by day that winter I would sneak into the empty house, roam its wood floors, five bedrooms, three baths, amiable sunroom, and paneled library. I dreamed it into my life.

Both houses were built in 1938, but the new one was expansive, with windows everywhere and L-shapes and niches and nooks. Unlike the upright colonial — an orderly valedictorian, a good girl — this house invited openness and surprise. It is a woman of the world at ease in her chemise.

And miraculously, we were able to buy it on a short sale, as it turned out, for $71,000 cash. This is the Flint of this century, where the average home price is about $45,000. This is the Flint that torments realtors and rewards those who find themselves at anchor here. We can have homes like this.

De Botton says, "When buildings talk, it is never with a single voice. Buildings are choirs rather than soloists; they possess a multiple nature from which arise opportunities for beautiful consonance as well as dissension and discord."

From the beginning, I'm serious, Maxine #2 sang to me—a sensuous hum, a nurturing welcome, motherly in its calming resonance.

Its history, like Flint's, has its share of dissonance. Andrew Highsmith documents Flint's racist real estate past well in his book *Demolition Means Progress: Flint, Michigan, and the Fate of the American Metropolis*. Like most of the houses in "better" neighborhoods, this one would have had a deed restriction like one he documents that read "no property within the above description shall be sold, leased, assigned or transferred, or any interest therein, to any person or persons other than those belonging to the Caucasian race."

That's one part of living on Maxine Street that unsettles. Seventy years ago, it was populated only by white people who complicitly enabled discrimination. I am trying to exercise humility in the face of this history, and I am relieved that now the neighborhood can be, and is, more diverse.

That history wasn't the house's fault. This is the home where I now abide, the place that makes me so happy every morning when I come down to that sunny kitchen. Its graceful spaces invariably resolve my angst and calm my fears.

It is a quieter life now. My husband doesn't drink and I've lost my taste for partying. I am satisfied to spend time walking, thinking, writing, watching the backyard birds, trying to be a good friend.

Within the shelter of some of Flint's best houses, I seem to have found my adulthood. I arrived in Flint a restless young woman, and now I'm old. But not unhappy, even in this troubled town. Its houses, so many still standing tall, some graced with vestigial elegance, offer succor and reassurance. They remind us we too can endure.

Fresh to Death

ERIC WOODYARD

ay stepped into Arlene's Nightclub fresh to death on a chilly Sunday night in October.

He was clean as hell, rocking a pair of flashy True Religion jeans and burgundy Bally sneakers, with a tan sweater trimmed in matching burgundy. The words "Trouble Man" were stamped across his chest.

A flock of fine ass chicks trailed his smooth cologne scent. From the outside looking in, he was a true baller.

He stood near the bar, with his homie Duke, sending shot-after-shot to the loosest females in the building. By the end of the night, he was setting up a play for the baddest of them all.

Duke and Tay were the local promoters of the comedy show happening at Arlene's. Ciroc Boi Entertainment was their official tag.

Tay was my brother. We weren't related by blood, but Tay was truly like family to me. He was a devoted father, son, brother, hustler, and a certified mack. You'd rarely ever catch him stepping out to a club or bar and not looking fly—even if he was just popping in for a split second. He grew up down the street, near both of my grandmothers on the nutty north side of town. I met him so early in life that I really can't remember any formal introduction. His aura reminded me of legendary boxing champion Floyd Mayweather with his slight stutter and bright smile. Tay could light up any room. I had a lot of love for that dude, and whenever we stepped out together I was guaranteed to have a fun time. But on the night of the comedy show I was chilling at my mom's house because my body had shut down from excessive alcohol consumption throughout the week. I'll leave it at that. I needed to get my black ass mentally prepared for work the next morning and I couldn't take a chance at partying too hard with Tay that night. Duke and Tay had flown in a comedian from Washington D.C. as the headline act, but even with a modest crowd, the show still had to go on.

Unfortunately, the bulk of the folks—looking to drink and party—didn't arrive until after the comedian's set had already ended. But Tay and Duke still showed the comedian love and blessed him with a portion of their earnings from the door. Tay kept the jokester's cup filled with vodka shots, too. Shit was all good.

By two a.m. the countless Ciroc shots and Bud Ice beer started to kick in.

Everybody at Arlene's was feeling a good buzz as they headed for the doorway. Tay and Duke even lined up a few chicks to come home with them, but there was one problem: The liquor store was closed.

As the owners shut down Arlene's, Tay and Duke were among the last ones to leave. Tay skirted off recklessly. He punched at least sixty miles per hour on the dashboard down North Saginaw Street in his white 2007 Dodge Charger. Tay was headed to an after-hours spot to grab another fifth of Ciroc. Duke took off in the opposite direction in his green truck to get gas before entertaining the women.

Wandering closely near the door of the after-hours spot were a couple of strange-looking black dudes, according to an eyewitness who I promised would stay anonymous. One was tall and light skinned and the other was a muscular, dark-skinned guy with a thick beard.

Tay knocked on the door, then gave the guys dap as he waited to get in.

"Wassup, my nigga!" Tay greeted them.

"Are they charging in there, my nigga?" one asked.

"Probably a couple of dollars, if that," Tay said. "You just gotta buy some drinks."

"Man, I ain't buying no drinks," the other guy said. "Is they searching?"

"Yeah, they're gonna pat you down or something," Tay explained as they walked back toward the door.

As Tay banged on the door again, the light-skinned guy exposed a handgun.

"You know what, man, run that shit." he told Tay.

"Y'all niggas are gonna try to rob me?" Tay asked.

"Run that motherfucking shit before I kill you," he repeated.

Tay placed his hands on the door with a gun pointed toward his head as the dark-skinned guy ran his pockets.

"That's fucked up that y'all niggas robbing me like this." Tay shook his head in disbelief.

"Shut the fuck up before I pop you," the tall guy yelled.

Tay beat on the door again before it finally flew open. He ran in, explained the situation, and raced back out to spot the thieves. The duo was still in the same spot. As soon as the robbers saw Tay coming back out, they fired.

Tay's body collapsed on the hard concrete as soon as the bullet entered his left temple. A stream of blood flowed from his head onto the street as paramedics arrived on the scene. His clothes were soaked in blood.

"Oh, my God, Tay!" a woman screamed. "Talk to me."

He never recovered. Two days later, Tay took his last breath, on October 22, 2013, at Hurley Medical Center. He was thirty-two years old. The news hit me like a shockwave.

I'll never forget that day. I was lying in bed, chilling with my pregnant girlfriend, when my mother barged in the room to deliver the news.

"Tay just died," she yelled.

I jumped out of bed in disbelief. Tay and I had been hanging out that entire week in celebration of my twenty-fifth birthday. In fact, I was right at that same after-hours spot that he got shot in front of just four days before the incident.

What if I had decided to attend that comedy show with him that Sunday night? I would've likely trailed him to get a bottle of liquor. Would those guys have shot me, too? Maybe I wouldn't be here, either. That's a scary thought but a truthful one. To make matters worse, Tay's girlfriend was also pregnant with his unborn daughter. He couldn't wait to father his third child. We discussed fatherhood that entire week.

"Can you believe that this gonna be my first baby that I'll be out of the joint to raise from day one?" Tay kept saying, smiling. "That shit crazy."

"It's gonna be wild," I said, as we passed around a bottle of Ciroc. "Our babies will be tight since they're so close in age."

"I know," he told me. "If it's a boy, I'm gonna name him after me but if it's a girl her name will be Dessiah."

Tay never got a chance to even learn the baby's gender. Maybe someday I can tell Dessiah how cool her Daddy was.

Moving on the streets of Flint in the late night can be deadly. It took for me to lose Tay to really grasp this. In the daytime, many people identify me as Eric Woodyard, award-winning sports reporter, but at night people see me differently. There was once a time where I partied nearly every night. In fact, I still like to go out, but I'm way more cautious of my surroundings. Stepping in any club around Flint, especially the hood ones, you have to be prepared to encounter some bullshit. It's really that serious. Anything can break out.

That tension hangs in the air in my life to this day. It's a weird line that I have to walk—between downtown corporate Flint and where I was raised, between night and day, between the two different identities I've formed. There's that side of me that likes to live on the edge and then there's the responsible father that excels in his career. To keep it plain and simple, I try to resolve that tension by using Tay as an example when I feel that I'm going overboard.

Growing up in the Fifth Ward of Flint, there weren't many places around town where I didn't feel comfortable. When you aren't bothering anybody or involved in any illegal activity, why would you be afraid of going anywhere? But in Flint, trouble can still manage to find you by being in the wrong place at the wrong time.

Tay was like me. He went out a lot. He drank lots of liquor. He messed around with women. Life was fun for Tay. He lived single and carefree.

I still remember walking into the newsroom the next day after Tay was shot. Somehow, I kept my composure and didn't mention it to anyone on the job for fear of them asking me to connect a reporter with the family. That was way too close to my comfort zone to assist anyone with sources for that. The headline on the article written by one of my close coworkers read: "One man in critical condition after shooting at Flint bar, suspect in custody." Later in the week it was updated to: "Man dies after being shot outside Flint nightclub." To them, Tay's death was just one of fifty-two homicides in 2013. Four more folks were murdered after him in the city that year. Flint's death toll was actually its lowest total since 2009, but all it takes is to lose one person and the statistics go out of the window.

As sad as it was for me and my family to lose Tay to senseless violence, it also taught me a valuable lesson.

Sometimes life isn't fair and when it's your time to go then it's your time. You can't beat death. Tay wasn't bothering anybody when those guys gunned him down. Being fresh to death in Flint could literally be your cause of death.

Rest in peace, Deonta Blackmon.

ERIC WOODYARD

No Pawnshops for Old Stories

TEDDY ROBERTSON

Note: An earlier version of this essay appeared in the online edition of Flint's East Village Magazine.

I turn the key in the lock of the kitchen door and gaze distractedly through the lowest panes of its nine-lite window. A slight but unaccustomed disorder in the dining room. Chairs at an oblique angle to the table, the rug somewhat crooked. Now that I've walked in, why are the winter draft rolls in the middle of the room? The hall door to the upstairs unaccountably open? No one seems to be here, but I feel a sense of someone having rushed by rapidly. I call out my son's name questioningly—the only other person with a house key and who might enter at any time. Maybe an emergency search for tools or auto parts still socked away in attic and garage?

And then it hits me; someone else has been in my house.

I stare, hypnotized, at details not yet part of a picture, like a gawker at a highway accident. Treading carefully through my own house as if not to disturb it more, I move from the dining room, through the hall to the bedroom. Why are the dresser drawers open, underwear and socks rising like yeasty bread dough overflowing the sides of a baking pan?

Of course: this is where ladies' loot might be tucked into little private places, or nestled in sateen-lined boxes with lids that snap shut, or laid out in the efficient squares and rectangles of the burgundy faux-felt compartments that organize everything.

On top of the mahogany dresser sits the pottery dish where each night I dropped the jewelry most a part of me. Empty. Pearl earrings received at college graduation, my dad's signet ring, a watch fob from my grandfather made into a pendant. A pinkie ring made from an uncle's stickpin. What else had been there just hours ago? Each piece was bound to a family story. Everything was old, laden with memories. Only this morning gold chains had been tangled in the dish, linking my life to those now dead but daily remembered.

I reach out but can't touch the disarray, its surfaces tender like a wound. I retrace my steps and exit, but this time through the front door. I need to tell someone that my things are gone, grabbed in haste by someone who did not know them. I stride with purpose across the street, ring my neighbor's bell, and blurt out my distress. She and her daughter are more alarmed; could someone still be in the house? We call the police and then return to the crime scene my bedroom has become. A kind of postmortem begins, though the body is gone.

I live in Flint, in the city limits, a mere twenty minutes from my job on the University of Michigan-Flint campus. My neighborhood, Mott Park, flourished in the 1950s when my house was built. The day of the robbery it's October and the weather is still mild—no rain or snow. But days are short; I've returned home in twilight.

The next morning I sit at the dining room table, trying to list the missing items, to describe their shapes, name their materials, and estimate their ages. Price out their values. Their identities derive from their history—each piece had belonged to someone else before it came to me. In my grandfather's time, gentlemen wore stickpins and had monogrammed watch fobs; they carried small penknives, engraved with their initials, relatively useless but hallmarks of elegance in 1920s New York. Fresh sorrows emerge as lost pieces come to mind that I hadn't remembered initially.

Unlike princes and warriors of the ancient world, we are not buried with our treasure; our grave goods are handed down. My grandmother and mother would give me some small piece for an important birthday, a coming of age gift. Closing their tale of a ring or pin I admired, they would say to me, "You may have this when you are older." And so it was that the story melded to the object. A ring or a bracelet marked my passage from childhood, to adolescence, to graduation, to marriage. I too, in turn, had small pieces that just lay in the drawer, waiting for another young woman, perhaps a daughter-in-law, to grow into them.

The household insurance did not cover what was gone; I had not lost enough, it seemed. The agent needed valuations in the thousands. I took my list to the Flint police station, where the sergeant, impatient and patronizing, had much more serious, life-and-death issues in his office distant from the front desk. I should just leave my list of items with the somnolent clerk behind the cage. In any case, the goods were probably long since out of the area, on their way to Detroit. Pawnshops might help—although they aren't supposed to deal with hot goods—but I could take my list around to them.

Steeled by loss, I set off for the local pawnshops, their locations vaguely recalled because I had disdained them, never stopped to look inside. I am humbled now as I timidly enter Mega Pawn, Diane's, and the Music Box. Weaving through dusty tunnels of tools and TVs at the entrances, I make my way to the back and the jewelry counter. The clerks vary. One takes my list to the backroom, perhaps smokes a cigarette and returns: "no descriptions match." Another, more conversational, confides that he has so much jewelry in the back safe that every three weeks some of the stuff is just shipped off to be melted down. Once chosen with care, engraved, presented as gifts marking important occasions, my family jewelry might return eventually to its original state. Bullion. A fate more appalling than theft. Sold at market price, recast into ingots, my family jewelry could simply revert to its elemental state and rejoin the world supply of precious metal.

A neighbor tried to console me with urban lore. Every once in a while, a local drug bust turns up a cache of stolen jewelry. The stuff never makes it to pawn at all. Dealers hoard it, give it to favored women; the goods are traded internally. Just hang in there and wait, he counseled.

It's been several years now since the break-in. From time to time, I stop in at the pawn shops in Flint, following clerks' advice that the stock in the cases changes every few months. I'm almost a regular. I've adjusted to the dim light, the dusty displays. Now comfortable, I slowly walk the cases. Bending over the glass, I see bracelets and necklaces, mostly gold, their designs clichéd and rarely distinctive; perhaps their lack of originality makes them easy to move on the pawn market. Twelve to fourteen feet of wedding ring sets arrayed in rows, the rank and file of failure. Engagement rings with sad, small stones; the purchaser could afford little, but wanted to be proper. The recipient was thrilled at the new stage of life that this tiny diamond signified. But now, through disappointment or desperation, it's in pawn along with the wedding band. Sadder stories than my own.

Some of my losses I can still visualize quite clearly, their color, engraving, some detailed filigree, or how a ring felt on my finger. Thinking of the objects fondly, I wish that I could tell their stories to the new possessors—it's the stories that can still pierce my chest.

Few pieces remain, but I wait to pass down what is left. With their stories, of course; that's the most important part.

The Spirit of Sam Jones

BOB CAMPBELL

S tanding tall in the heart of Flint's downtown are monuments to the city's celebrated past. William C. Durant. David Buick. Louis Chevrolet. Albert Champion. You know them by the companies they created—Buick, Chevrolet, AC Spark Plug, and, of course, General Motors. And, believe it or not, they all ran the streets at one time or another in Flint, Michigan.

Flint—the birthplace of General Motors—was once home to the greatest concentration of GM factories in the world. At its peak, GM employed about 80,000 people. Like many who grew up in Flint, I had family and friends who all had family sprinkled across GM's vast industrial landscape here.

My father and brother worked at AC. (Eventually, I would be employed there, too, first as a high school co-op student and then later as a skilled tradesman.) Over at Chevrolet is where neighborhood friends Mark and Jeff's father worked. And Fisher Body is where Butchie and Bo's father worked. Then there was Buick, where my Aunt Marion had an office job at the old division headquarters.

The abundance of industrial might and wealth also made Flint a key weapon in the nation's Arsenal of Democracy during World War II. Later, during the Cold War, we took it as a morbid badge of honor that our city was likely very high on the Soviet Union's target list if there were ever a nuclear exchange. In fact, my father said he had prepared to evacuate the family from Flint to our cottage in the Thumb during the height of the Cuban missile crisis.

So these automotive pioneers not only put Flint on the map but did much to help define the American Century. Thus, it's understandable that you'd find statues of them—Durant, Buick, Chevrolet, and Champion—in the General Motors Automotive Pioneer Plaza on the city's main street. They're legends, with stories about them told over and over.

Among the giants on Saginaw Street in downtown Flint stands my Uncle Melton. Chances are you won't see him. But I can assure you, he's there. His contributions to building this city are far less understood but here's what I can tell you.

His name wasn't really Melton—his legal name, that is. It was Sam. Sam Jones. How Melton Eaton became Sam Jones is also the stuff of legends, a walk through the history of a city where he (and men like him) made his presence known.

To a child, Uncle Melton was a large, barrel-chested man with wide shoulders. In a 1956 black-and-white photograph—when he would have been nearly sixty years old—he still had the bearing of a prizefighter.

His voice was husky and loud for no reason at all in that way of men who had worked many years on the factory floor. When Uncle Melton thundered, "Hey, Bobby," I didn't know whether to run and hide or not. Usually, he was just saying hello, but it sounded authoritarian, frightening.

He was a dark man, too. That he always seemed to be dressed in a white T-shirt and dark trousers, and seated in the muted daylight of his living room, only served to accentuate his ebony complexion.

I don't ever recall seeing him laugh or smile broadly. He seemed to have the perpetual glare of a serious man—not that he was a mean or angry person. He was a retired working man who was, perhaps, more than a little set in his ways and protective of all that he had accomplished.

When I knew him, he and his wife, Addie Mae, lived on Park Street. The white, two-story Cape Cod, a common style of residential architecture in Flint, had burgundy window awnings and shutters.

The house sat within old Floral Park, a well-established residential enclave on Flint's south side that bordered downtown. The area was home to a great cross-section of working-class, merchant-class, and professional people who happened to be black. (Way back in the day, a Lansing native named Malcolm Little was said to have spent quite a bit of time in the Floral Park community, too, in the years before he became Malcolm X.)

Uncle Melton's home always felt different than ours. Devoid of brats running about, it was serene, with that plastic-covered living room furniture and that tan double box fan sitting on the floor that never seemed to be on. And I was certain that he raised chickens because whenever we visited, mama or daddy always left with a dozen or so eggs. But my sisters and I never spotted any chickens during our brief visits to his house. There wasn't a chicken coop tucked behind the home; just a regular ol' backyard with grass, some shrubs, and a shade tree.

The house on Park Street still stands today even though most of Floral Park was all but erased to make way for the I-69/I-475 interchange, a controversial urban renewal project—one of the hundreds of transportation infrastructure projects in cities across the country used to eliminate black residential neighborhoods perceived to be slums by government and city officials. Though the memories are vague, I can still recall the thrill of seeing bulldozers and other heavy construction equipment clearing huge swaths of land just north of Uncle Melton's Park Street home while still too young to appreciate all the history and memories that were also being hauled away in those great big dump trucks.

Melton Eaton was born 1898 in Mobile, Alabama. He shared the same birth year as my paternal grandfather, who was raised in Georgia. Both men came to Michigan, albeit separately, during the Great Migration of blacks from the South that began in the 1910s. A former sharecropper, Grandpa moved North sometime after 1923, bringing with him a young wife and two small children, including my father. They settled in the old St. John Street neighborhood that once stood where I-475 and hundreds of acres of a largely vacant industrial park exist today.

Uncle Melton's migration story is less clear. But I am quite certain he came North, like many of his contemporaries, in search of better wages, a chance to own property, a right to vote, perhaps, and a more dignified existence. Along with the new challenges and opportunities, many of the blacks who settled in Flint would also encounter Michigan's particularly nasty brand of discrimination and segregation.

As a young reporter for the *Flint Journal* in 1993, I had chronicled the story of such men, who had fled the economically depressed and racially oppressive South to settle in places like Flint where there was a demand for workers to meet the needs of the city's rapidly expanding automobile factories. The labor shortage was exacerbated by the drop in European immigration, which was halted during World War I. Many white Southerners also migrated to the industrial North during this time.

One man I interviewed was ninety-one-year-old J.D. Dotson. Dotson, who retired from General Motors in 1967 after forty-four years, told me that GM would send "man-catchers" south to find able-bodied men to work in the factories.

"They would be brought up here, free, in box cars from Cincinnati," said Dotson, who was born in Flint in 1901.

Dotson started at Flint's massive Buick complex in 1923 as a laborer in the foundry division. "Every 'other' job I applied for, I was told 'it' was a white man's job," he said.

Another man I interviewed, Oscar Barnett, quit his job at an Arkansas sawmill after the owner refused to give him a raise, saying "Ain't a n----- in the world worth $100 a week." So, in 1953, Barnett relocated to Flint, hitching a ride with the "Robinson boys—T.J. (Thomas J.) and Leon—[who] were boot-legging boys up here." Barnett found work at the Buick foundry, too, and soon learned that he could send about $100 week to his wife back in Arkansas by working overtime.

But the money was anything but easy.

"Oh man … it was hot," he told me. "When I started, the foreman said, 'I'm going to put you on the merry-go-round.' The only merry-go-rounds I heard of were at the carnival."

The "merry-go-round" was a large turntable fitted with brake-drum molds, and his job was to pour molten iron into the cavities between machine cycles.

Uncle Melton also worked in the Buick foundry. Prior to WW II, and for a time afterwards, the foundry, custodial work, and other such jobs were among the few positions open to black men in the industry. He retired in 1965. I have no idea whether Uncle Melton worked on the "merry-go-round" inside the Buick foundry or not. I also do not know his mode of travel from Alabama to Michigan and if a "man-catcher" was involved in his travel arrangements.

However, I do know that it was sometime after his retirement—the late '60s or very early '70s—when he rescued a neighbor from a house ablaze on Park Street. His heroics even earned him an interview with the *Flint Journal*. To prepare, he did what you'd expect a man of his generation would do. Uncle Melton put on a suit and a pair of sunglasses to conduct the interview.

His heroism and interview preparation became part of family lore. I tried, without success, to locate the *Flint Journal* article about his actions on that day for this piece. I even enlisted the help of the collections curator at Sloan-Longway Museum, where the *Journal* archives—the so-called morgue, in newspaper speak—are now housed. Though quite helpful, the curator finally reported back to me several days later what I had discovered on my own, searching the microfilm collection at the Flint Public Library: "Without the date or a clipping file, I am afraid we would be stuck searching through each page of the paper from the years you mentioned," he wrote to me via email.

Maybe there was never an article written about him. Or if there was, maybe it was nothing more than a news brief with the individuals never identified by name. [e.g., "A man yesterday rescued a man (or) a woman (or) a child from a house fire on Park Street in Flint. The victim was treated for smoke inhalation. The house sustained minor damage. In other news…"] After all, no one died and the house wasn't destroyed. So I can imagine the city editor's reaction when the reporter returned to the newsroom: "That's it? It's a brief."

But the rescue story, confirmed by my much-older sister and brother (both teenagers at the time), lives on. That missing piece of documented history is symbolic, too. It fits well within the African-American oral tradition of handing down stories from generation to generation because journalists and historians at the time weren't as likely to record the history of black people, who were considered outside the "mainstream." It's also emblematic of a man who was there even if there's no record of it.

Still, it wasn't his only selfless act that went largely unknown outside the family.

Uncle Melton wasn't really my uncle. He was actually my mother's first cousin, making him my cousin, once removed. For a time, he shared a house with my maternal grandmother, mother, and aunt on Liberty and later Wellington streets in Floral Park. Known as "doubling up," this was a common living arrangement among black residents in Flint and elsewhere because of housing shortages related to racial segregation.

When I asked my mother why we called him Uncle Melton, she said it was because he was old enough to be her father. And as far as I know, he never had any children of his own.

Second, when Uncle Melton died in 1973 at St. Joseph Hospital, it happened on December—Pearl Harbor Day. Thirty-one years earlier on that same day—a year to-the-date after the day of infamy—my father was inducted into the U.S. Army and went on to become a decorated combat veteran in Italy during World War II.

I was just nine years old when mama got off the phone and announced that Uncle Melton had died. Although he had been sick for some time, the closing of an era had already begun. Automotive pioneer and philanthropist Charles Stewart Mott—one of Flint's most powerful corporate and civic leaders—had passed away just ten months earlier in February. Melton's death also occurred in the midst of the first Arab Oil Embargo, which sent the price of oil through the roof and caused gasoline shortages nationwide, and dealt the first of several body blows to the city's main industry.

Meanwhile, funeral preparations began in earnest for Uncle Melton. However,

when his brief obituary was published in the *Flint Journal* days later, the name
"Melton Eaton" was nowhere to be found.

There were the familiar names of "Wife, Addie Mae"; two brothers, "W.C. Eaton
(Effie) of Mobile, Alabama and S. Mack (Henrietta) of Luskin, Texas"; and "2
nieces, Mr. and Mrs. Clarence (Rose) Campbell and Mr. and Mrs. Shed (Marion)
Hudspeth all of Flint" in the write-up. But the name at the top read: Sam Jones.

"Why is Uncle Melton called Sam Jones?" I asked family members. "Who is
Sam Jones?"

With the slightest hint of a smile, my father, in a response directed at my mother,
replied: "Tell him."

Mama proceeded to explain.

"When your Uncle Melton went to get a job at Buick, the person doing the hir-
ing looked at him and said: 'What's your name? Sam?'

"Melton replied, 'Yeah!'

"The guy said, 'Oh… Sam what?'

"'Jones. Sam Jones.'"

Sam. It was a racial jab, no doubt; the name most likely shorthand for "Sambo"
or "Little Black Sambo," a derogatory term for blacks common to the era.

Uncle Melton counterpunched—making it clear that he was nobody's dummy
and nobody's punk—and left with a promising factory job.

I can believe it, too. For me, that '56 photo of him standing tall and erect in that
double-breasted suit says it all.

Eventually, his legal name became Sam Jones. In doing so, he took the derogatory slur and made it into a dignified name with a paycheck to boot.

But within the family, he would be forever known as Melton.

I distinctly recall my mother's undeniable affection for Uncle Melton. He was
something of a father figure for her, especially since her parents had divorced when
she was a small child. And, although he never told me, I'm certain that my father
shared my mother's fondness for him, too. The reasons, I think, stem in part from
a shared experience that one comes to appreciate with age. Their experiences were
not the same, but they came from a familiar place.

My father was working as a janitor at the old AC plant on Industrial Avenue
when fear spread after the Japanese had bombed Pearl Harbor. When he returned
home from the war in 1946, daddy went back to AC and was promptly handed a
mop and pail. But the former staff sergeant, who had earned his stripes, Combat
Infantryman Badge, and Bronze Star fighting Nazis in the segregated U.S. Army,

said no thanks. Daddy instead "took the dirtiest, filthiest job" at AC, which involved moving a train car of scrap metal manually using a handcar, because he said he wanted something more than janitorial work. He felt he had earned it.

Uncle Melton was like that, too. He was a man of his times. He put in his years of service and did what he was felt was necessary to acquire a better life for himself and those for whom he cared, to secure his slice of the American Dream in a booming industrial Mecca.

As Flint strives to remake itself from the remnants of itself former self, I wonder what crosses people's minds when they see the statues of automotive pioneers on Saginaw Street? Or when they recall the '36-'37 Sit-Down Strike that gave birth to the United Auto Workers. I wonder how they picture Flint in its "heyday."

For me, the usable past contains far more than those individuals immortalized downtown. It also embraces Uncle Melton, whose fighting and enduring spirit helped build the city and drives it still. His soul lives on, not unlike the countless other men who helped build Flint and whose presence demanded respect.

Though you don't see any statues of men like Melton Eaton, aka Sam Jones, in downtown Flint, he was a giant, nonetheless. Standing there on Saginaw Street, I can assure you, he's there.

Flintlock

STEPHANIE CARPENTER

After my doorbell chimed in the middle of the night, I asked my landlord to give me more locks. I lived alone then in the front half of an old house in Flint, Michigan. I'd moved to town to teach creative writing in August 2010, two weeks after the apprehension of a serial stabber. He wouldn't have wanted me, that killer: a six-foot-five Israeli-Arab, he targeted small-framed black men, not skinny white women. Late at night, he'd find such men walking alone and ask for directions or help with his car. The serial stabber worked Genesee County for three months before being apprehended on his way back to Israel, by a gate agent at the Atlanta airport. I lived a few blocks from the university, in a neighborhood recommended by the campus cops. Still, I feared what the stabber suggested about Flint's police force. I'd heard of people dying of asthma attacks because Flint's first responders were too slow. If someone broke into my apartment, I would dial 911 and I would dial my Vietnam combat-veteran landlord, but I believed that escape would be my best defense.

I knew all the ways someone could break into my apartment. The front and side entrances were daunting, well-fortified with steel security doors and motion-sensing lights. But from the living and dining rooms, French doors opened onto a wide porch. Though sealed shut and double-hung, those doors were nevertheless walls made of glass. The door from the kitchen to the basement was even more fragile, hollow-core with a turn-button lock. My landlord and his handyman sometimes came into my apartment through the basement; there was no point of egress on my side, so I knew that there must be an exterior door somewhere beyond the repurposed bi-fold closet doors that separated my part of the basement from my neighbor's. Had the last person out made sure to lock up?

Then there were the windows. In New Orleans, I'd heard tell, bold housebreakers carried ladders. Why not in Flint? The porch roof peaked directly beneath my bedside window, offering a way in or out. I dreaded the clang of rungs against gutter. But if the stairs caught on fire, or if I heard someone climbing them, I planned to crawl out that window, dragging my comforter with me. I would throw the comforter onto the evergreen beside the porch and then throw myself after it, sinking fifteen feet through branches and blanket until I touched the ground.

At times that apartment felt vulnerable—at others, impregnable. I'd always liked living alone; this was even more true in Flint. After a full day on campus, I liked coming home to a quiet I controlled. On Saturdays, I liked listening to the radio while I put up food for the week. I used pioneer language like "put up" to refer to the tasks of washing lettuce or making bread from bananas I couldn't finish fast enough. Serious cookery was beyond me. Still, I felt purposeful and self-contained, preparing popcorn dinners for just myself. I drew a decent paycheck from the university and my rent was low. For the first time in my life I wasn't worried about money: I could afford new clothes for my new job as a professor, make payments on my student loans, and start a savings account. My apartment was cheap but spacious enough for an office, a bedroom, and a guest room besides. I was ready to receive what visitors might come. My sister came; a friend from high school. Some weekends, my partner. But most of the time, I was glad to be alone and independent. In the evenings I would turn on the remote-controlled electric log in the dining room fireplace. I would pull one of my pink vinyl dinette chairs to the hearth, brace my feet above the fake flame, and write.

But when my doorbell chimed in the middle of the night it reminded me that I wasn't really alone. There were people outside of my apartment, some of whom I did not want to invite inside. The houses on either side of mine were owned by my landlord and filled with tenants he'd vetted: students, professionals, his own brother. The homeowners across the street were fanatical about lawn care and vigilant with pleasantries. At the top of our street still lined with actual iron hitching posts was a house zoned for horses. It had a stable out back and—before he disgraced himself, by overturning Santa's sleigh at the Christmas parade—a young Percheron grazing out front. A retirement home stood at the top of the street; a Victorian bed-and-breakfast in the middle. But kitty-corner to my place, men with long grey hair drank and argued all day on their porch sofa. G., who delivered drugs from a yellow house four doors down, would visit that porch at intervals. If I happened to be on my porch, he'd stop afterward to say hi.

I'd met G. walking home one night after teaching my evening class. A small-framed black man, he was more vulnerable than I was to certain threats. Still, I'd been scared when he fell into step beside me in the dark, at the edge of campus. As we walked together, toward the same block of the same street, I schemed—as I sometimes did in my apartment—as to what I'd do if the situation escalated. But he only asked me questions: how tall was I, what did I teach, where was I staying? G. was in his mid-thirties, like me, but his hair and teeth were sparse and I wasn't surprised to learn that he stayed at the yellow house. He was carrying home take-out for his old lady; he said he was concerned to see me walking by myself. After that night, we often chatted in passing. G. would propose plans for us: a trip to the Red Lobster, a visit to the planetarium, a bottle of Riunite followed by a ride on our neighbor's Harley. If he saw me in running clothes, he'd suggest that we jog together on the track of the neighborhood's shuttered high school. As a writer, I appreciated the specificity of his suggestions; as a woman living alone, I appreciated their ephemerality. His were always someday plans, safe for being so.

G. never rang my doorbell or intentionally sought me out, but I told myself it was most likely him, that late night when the bell woke me. Instead of answering the door, I'd called my landlord. He came immediately, patrolled the premises. No one was around. No one likely meant any harm, ringing the bell rather than breaking a window or launching a ladder. But my landlord respected my fears: what if? What if someone had been assessing the place before breaking in? My landlord installed a deadbolt in the door at the top of the stairs, a deadbolt in my bedroom door. These meant that I could stop wedging chairs under doorknobs at night and setting booby-traps. The heavy oak doors on the second floor were original to the house; an intruder would need an axe to get through them. In the meantime I could be out my bedroom window with my blanket parachute and my landlord could be running in a combat crouch through our conjoined backyards. I felt safer for having more locks. If I still lay awake some nights listening, if I still got out of bed to press my ear to the floorboards, it was because I knew that there was no such thing as impenetrability. Locks are one thing; vigilance is better. Neither is infallible.

I gave up that apartment in August 2013. I gave up that life—which I loved—and moved into a house with my partner, in a small northerly town where no one ever locks their doors. Visitors let themselves in; solicitors sometimes, too. In our shared house, my office is my own: an attic that my partner renovated just for me, with my books all around and adult furniture that I bought using my Flint paychecks. There's no lock on the door that leads up narrow stairs to the room where I try to write. Knock before you come up, I've asked, over and over again—and sometimes he does. The difference between a landlord and a lover is that one will give you all the locks you ask for, while the other is wounded by your wanting them. I have not lost the habit of listening for intruders; I will never feel comfortable in a place where people can walk in at will.

On my last day in Flint, G. stopped by. My partner was outside with the full U-Haul; I was inside sweeping. She's in the house, I heard my partner say. Go in and say goodbye. Would I have issued the same invitation? I don't remember what exactly G. said to me in my empty living room. He kissed me on the cheek; he told me he'd miss me. But I will not forget what he said to my partner. Take her home, he advised, and make love to her like a possum on a hound dog. It was the least sexy simile I'd ever heard. It was also nothing G. would have said to me directly. We tended to talk about my teaching, or how his family had wronged him, or his plans to enroll in welding classes at the community college. I'm so depressed, G continued. I'm going to go home and do some cocaine. I'm confident that no one else has ever reacted to my leaving in that way—nor would I wish for it. But G's candor was what surprised me most about Flint, and it was something I experienced with neighbors, students, cab drivers, strangers. For as many locks as there are in that town, and for as much as we all relied on them, people in Flint can be incredibly unguarded. In one of the most dangerous cities in America, a psychopath could lure grown men with a tired story about car trouble; in that same city, a writer could gather material just by listening. This culture of openness seemed to me like both a liability and a defense system—connection as a means of self-protection. That culture made me feel at home in Flint as I rarely have elsewhere, despite being constitutionally incapable of returning people's confidences in kind.

In Flint I enjoyed the privilege of taking care of myself, comfortably. I lived there after the worst of the 2010 arsons, after the serial stabber, before the water went bad. I lived there during an interval when it seemed as though locks, diligence, and goodwill could protect me from anything, and nothing happened in those three years to disprove my fragile beliefs. I lived in Flint lightly, always aware of escape routes, and with the resources to choose between that life and some other. When I return now I regret that I've left—but I wonder what stories I'd be telling if I'd stayed.

City Beat: Covering Hoops in Basketball City USA

PATRICK HAYES

"T his must be your first city game."

At my first opportunity to ask a question on the Flint high school basketball beat in December 2008, I defaulted to the beloved crutch of the sportswriter—the question that's not really a question—and muttered something like "talk about the intensity of this game" to then-Flint Northwestern coach David Bush.

His innocent-but-condescending response was certainly accurate. In addition to being the whitest dude in the building, I was obviously nervous, not sure what to expect the first time I'd ever really even set foot in a city school in north Flint, a region where the city's serious issues with crime and poverty were undeniably present. In the postgame scramble for quotes after Northwestern's win over Flint Northern, I'd decided it would be best to take the obvious route and focus on a vague sports cliché so I didn't look completely out of my element or offend anyone. As an outsider trying to earn the trust of people I'd have to cover all season, I didn't want to make a confrontational first impression.

And, though a lazy way to lead off my story, the game was intense. The schools were crosstown rivals, each with proud histories of churning out dozens of Division I NCAA players, several of whom went on to successful professional basketball careers in the United States and abroad. Basketball in Flint, for the city's top players, provided an avenue for kids who grew up in poverty to see and earn a living in exotic places all over the world.

The 2008-09 versions of the city high school teams were filled with kids with the same aspirations as their decorated predecessors—earning college scholarships and, ultimately, the opportunity to get paid to play basketball in the NBA or overseas. That first game I'd covered was exactly as competitive as you'd expect under those circumstances, with players ferociously attacking the basket, taking full advantage of lax officiating to clutch and grab at every opportunity on defense, and feeding off of small but boisterous contingents of fans supporting each team in the stands.

What it wasn't, though, was good basketball. But as a new face in this environment, I certainly wasn't going to be the one to call attention to that fact. Neither
team had a player on its roster who was a Division I, let alone a professional, prospect. Neither coaching staff seemed to run any semblance of a cohesive offensive
or defensive system. The gym was half empty, something that would've once been
unheard of for a Northern-Northwestern game—it was common for City Series
games in Flint to sell out in previous generations.

But I had no interest in writing about any of that. As a lifelong basketball fan
who had stumbled into sportswriting, in Flint, Michigan, there was no greater
beat in my mind than city hoops. Due to massive layoffs by my company, and to a
growing management directive that favored suburban coverage, I lucked my way
into a dream beat when my more experienced colleagues didn't want it. A minute
detail like declining talent didn't change the fact that I had more than a job—I was
entrusted with the stewardship of one of the city's most amazing resources, its
basketball legacy.

Flint, true to its underdog mentality, has an athletic tradition on par with much
larger talent pools in places like Chicago, Washington D.C., New York, and L.A.
The city has produced a Heisman Trophy winner, Olympic medalists, NBA and
MLB All-Stars, NFL All-Pros, members of NCAA, NBA, and NFL championship
teams, and players who, individually, have netted numerous other accolades at the
pro and college levels.

Serious issues including population loss, poverty, and crime (and, recently, a
state government-caused crisis resulting in high levels of lead in the water supply),
have had a significant impact on all aspects of life in Flint, including the city's
sports programs. But similar to the city itself, what remains in the athletic community is a captivating sense of pride in the past, and an unwavering resolve to reject a
fate as anything less than one of America's great sports cities.

I didn't cover championship-contending city teams. I didn't cover college-ready
city players. I didn't cover an abundant number of city coaches who—despite usually good intentions—made indelible impacts on the lives of young people as mentors
or leaders. Most often, what I encountered could be described as simply "struggle."
It manifested itself on a variety of scales, ranging from simple boredom to a lack of
vital resources to tough or abusive home lives to academic disinterest to dreams that
overshot realities to instances of real violence and tragedy.

But the biggest struggle was, simply, a group of kids naively and proudly determined to claim their place as part of a longstanding basketball legacy without any of the guidance, resources, or structure in place—vital resources in an environment as challenging as Flint—that previous generations enjoyed. Their stories wouldn't add decorated achievements and glories to Flint's basketball heritage. On the contrary, that heritage often proved to be a detriment as much as it was an inspiration—but they were every bit as powerful.

Defining Substance

Glen Rice is the greatest basketball player the city of Flint has ever produced. Rice was a member of championship teams in high school, college, and the NBA. He won the Mr. Basketball award in the state of Michigan in high school, was the Most Outstanding Player in a NCAA Tournament, was a three-time NBA All-Star, won an All-Star Game MVP, and even received a few votes for the NBA's Most Valuable Player award on two occasions.

Sure, there are other players who had decent NBA careers. Trent Tucker played with Michael Jordan and won a NBA championship. Morris Peterson had a lengthy and productive NBA career and is one of the most beloved players in the still-brief history of the Toronto Raptors. Terry Furlow is credited with recruiting Magic Johnson to Michigan State and his NBA career was off to a promising start before he was killed in a car accident in 1983. But Rice had the best professional career in the best professional league in the world—there's really no counter-argument if NBA success is the standard for determining a hierarchy of Flint's basketball greats.

But the thing is, there are counterarguments. They are passionate, occasionally heated, sometimes insane, and solely based on personal preferences of the beholder.

For a certain generation, former Flint Central point guard Eric Turner is the best the city has ever produced. Turner was a star of championship Central teams in the 1980s, and was a preview of how the point guard position would evolve in the modern game. Turner could certainly pass and run an offense, the vital and traditional functions of point guard play. But he was also typically the best scorer on the court, choosing when to be a distributor to get teammates involved and when to seek out his own shot.

And that shot of his is legendary. I was in an eighth grade gym class in my rural school district thirty minutes east of Flint, with no understanding of the city's basketball legacy, when I heard my first Eric Turner story. My gym teacher, a weekend warrior pickup basketball player at the YMCA in Flint who sometimes ran into Turner on the courts there, insisted Turner had never missed a shot in the hundreds of pickup games he'd witnessed him play. And this wasn't just typical sports hyperbole—he adamantly argued on multiple occasions that Eric Turner had not missed one shot in hundreds of pickup basketball games over several years.

If you're slightly younger, the best player Flint has ever produced is former Flint Northwestern scoring machine Cory Hightower. Hightower was a super athletic left wing famous for both his highlight reel plays during games and an equally highlight reel temper that often led to technical foul-inducing highlights every bit as entertaining as his basketball skills.

Turner and Hightower had similar career trajectories—both were second-round picks in the NBA draft who didn't stick in the league and went on to solid careers in professional leagues abroad. Both also have considerable mythologies that dwarf their career accomplishments.

Turner, an All-American at the University of Michigan, used to draw legitimate comparisons to Magic Johnson for his unique array of passing and scoring capabilities, manifesting in a distinguishable and charismatic style that earned him a legion of devoted followers in high school in the same fashion that Johnson did during his youth in Lansing. Turner even boasted his own Magic-esque nickname: "ET," a moniker he was given both for his initials and for his ability to "look one way and dish the other way" when passing.[1]

A who's-who of NBA players still remember Hightower as an elite talent. In an interview with *Flint Journal* sportswriter Eric Woodyard in 2009, former Detroit Piston Chucky Atkins—who had no connection to Flint other than his occasional summer appearances in the city's pro-am games when he was a member of the Pistons—remembered Hightower and noted that he should've been in the NBA upon learning that Woodyard was a Flint native.[2]

And, of course, it's impossible to mention Hightower's mythology without addressing the long-rumored reason he didn't last in the NBA. Hightower, a rookie in training camp with the Los Angeles Lakers, was allegedly cut after he refused his rookie duty of carrying bags for veteran players. And not just any veteran player—one of the greatest players in NBA history, Kobe Bryant.[3] Now, in subsequent years, High-

1   "Flint Star: The Greatest Player From Flint You've Never Heard Of." *Hebrews: 11:1*, May 24, 2006. Accessed: https://hebrews111.wordpress.com/2006/05/24/flint-star-the-greatest-player-from-flint-you%E2%80%99ve-never-heard-of/

2   Woodyard, Eric. "Interview: Chucky Atkins reminisces about his days in the Flint City Pro-Am." *It's Just Sports*, November 30, 2009. Accessed: http://blog.mlive.com/its-just-sports/2009/11/interview_chucky_at-kins_remini.html

3   Field, Jared. "Flint hoops legend, Cory Hightower, now coaching elementary school ball in Grand Blanc." *Flint Journal*, January 23, 2009. Accessed: http://blog.mlive.com/flintjournal/hotbedhoops/2009/01/flint_hoops_legend_cory_hightower_now_coaching_mid.html

tower has vehemently denied the accusation,[4] but it has undoubtedly aided the growth of his status as a local legend in Flint. And others have insisted that it's true, albeit with a different angry veteran inserted— Derek Harper instead of Kobe Bryant.[5]

Even Rice, in addition to his substantive on-court accomplishments, has quite the urban legend trailing him, involving a rumored one-night stand with a certain future candidate for Vice President during a tournament in Alaska as a member of the University of Michigan's basketball team.[6]

The neverending and impossible-to-settle debate about the greatest player the city of Flint has ever produced will never have a proper resolution. But the Turner-Rice-Hightower dialogue perfectly illustrates the vital characteristics of Flint basketball. Substance and career accomplishments matter. But equally important is the fact that Flint players are imprinted with a style and bravado that is unmistakably recognizable as its own distinct brand of "Flint Basketball" anywhere in the country. Those who embody that style, even if they don't measure up in overall career accomplishments, are every bit as beloved and important to the city's basketball mythology.

As interesting as the nuances, characters, and debates that make up the city's basketball history are, they're also maddening because no one bothered to write that shit down. For a reporter trying to piece together a complex history on the fly, trying to develop sources and trying to become an expert, it was done through an endless string of finding tidbits of interesting information, talking to people and, usually, being told of multiple others who had critical information living in their heads that I needed to track down.

The lack of a cohesive, documented Flint basketball history form is part of its appeal—the more information I was able to piece together, the more anecdotes I learned, the more I felt like I was part of an exclusive and elite club. Finding out more became an endless and obsessive quest.

---

4   Woodyard, Eric. "Catching Up With A Flint Legend: Cory Hightower Interview!" *Flintstones*, February 16, 2010. Accessed: https://eric32woodyard.wordpress.com/2010/02/16/catching-up-with-a-flint-legend-cory-hightower-interview/

5   Field, Jared. "My night in Lansing: Another Cory Hightower story to add to the list." *Hotbed Hoops*, February 4, 2009. Accessed: http://blog.mlive.com/flintjournal/hotbedhoops/2009/02/my_night_in_lansing_another_cory_hightower_story_t.html

6   Craggs, Tommy. "All The Details Of The Sarah Palin-Glen Rice Coitus You've Been Waiting For." *Deadspin*, September 19, 2011. Accessed: http://deadspin.com/5841835/all-the-details-of-the-sarah-palin-glen-rice-coitus-youve-been-waiting-for

The Artist

"Basketball to me is like poetry."[7]

Watching Flint Northwestern in the 2009-10 season, one player stood out from a purely artistic standpoint: Jaylen Magee. Magee was a strong but undersized wing player, capable of explosive bursts of energy and ability that made it impossible to ignore him on the court. He was crafty around the basket, using his strength and creativity to finish plays in traffic surrounded by bigger players. He was incredibly fast with the ball—combining purposeful and fluid motions with a quick first step to fly to the basket on breaks before defenses could settle. He had range on his jump shot that made it hard for defenses to play off of him, fearing his ability to fly by them to the rim if they got too close.

At its most basic level, basketball is a form of nonverbal expression. No two players approach the game the same way. Sports media obsesses over crowning the next Magic, the next Bird, the next Jordan, the next LeBron, and then all of a sudden Steph Curry comes along, dominating the game in a way that is completely different and reinventive compared to preceding "face of the NBA" players.

There's no rational way of explaining why individual styles resonate with some people and not others. But to an observer, the way Jaylen approached the game, used his natural abilities, and seemed to have a knack for picking the right times to unleash these explosive bursts of productivity just made sense. He was the first player that I watched in Flint who immediately inspired me to pursue a more in-depth profile.

I interviewed him sitting in the stands at Flint Southwestern High School while a junior varsity game was going on. Based on my previous experiences interviewing high school athletes, most are typically already versed in jock-speak from watching their favorite athletes give boring answers to even more boring questions on televised games. I wasn't expecting him to be very forthcoming the first time we really talked for more than a minute or two, but was caught off guard by his answer to my first question asking him how he would describe the way he plays.

He was able to connect what he did on the court with the abstract concept of athletics—particularly a sport as graceful and style-driven as basketball—as an art form. He freely compared his style of play with his interest in writing poetry. In my

---

7   Hayes, Patrick. "Northwestern's Jaylen Magee provides basketball team with offense in a variety of ways." *Flint Journal*, March 1, 2010. Accessed: http://highschoolsports.mlive.com/news/article/5246791207147543802/northwesterns-jaylen-magee-provides-basketball-team-with-offense-in-a-variety-of-ways/

sportswriting experiences, it was rare for a seventeen-year-old to make that sort of comparison—instead usually opting for unrealistic comparisons of themselves to superstar athletes, or just evading the question to talk about "the team" instead of their individual characteristics. In fact, most high school coaches I encountered had no ability to connect athletic pursuits to artistic ones.

Sports, particularly in urban settings, are taught as a means to an end. You play sports to earn scholarships, or to learn discipline, or to gain toughness. The fact that sports can, and should, feed creative or spiritual ambitions is rarely taught in youth sports.

As a failed athlete myself, I didn't gravitate toward and love basketball because I was hyperaggressive, or interested in proving my toughness, or filled with some pressing need to win and dominate. I love basketball because it's beautiful. The efforts of coaches who saw sports through the traditional lens never resulted in any meaningful takeaway for me from their limited interpretations of the value sports offer.

Meeting a kid like Jaylen in Flint was both rewarding and depressing. I felt an immediate connection with him because of his more thoughtful approach to the game, but also because of his wise-beyond-his-years ability to connect the development of his own style in terms that stretched beyond the typical jock-speak.

I was disappointed for him because of the lack of adults involved in sports who are able to nurture or even explain sports through that lens. A recurring theme with athletes in Flint is their fixation on sports as the only path out of the inner city, and the success of previous generations of athletes in Flint reinforces that belief. But, particularly now, with the talent pool significantly decreased as a result of population decline, without some modicum of academic performance, kids who receive athletic scholarships to universities big or small won't last long. What good is an athletic scholarship if you can't stay academically eligible?

Too often, academic shortcomings are overlooked because of a belief by many adults that taking sports away, even for poor grades or poor behavior in school, is taking away a kid's only viable path to success. In reality, they're doing the opposite—downplaying well-roundedness in favor of a fixation on sports alone, eroding other options when sports don't work out.

In Flint in the past, when there was an abundant talent supply and stable mentors in the athletic community, the single-minded pursuit of sports opportunities wasn't as detrimental. But when you remove some of that stability and when the talent level declines, you suddenly have a generation of kids with no backup plan, no passions or interests that have been nurtured other than sports, and what results are few-to-no options past high school.

Basketball didn't work out for Jaylen Magee as a path to a college or professional career. The reality is basketball is rarely a viable path to college for kids in the city of Flint anymore. The problem is the city's legacy that looms so large tells kids otherwise.

Defining "Flint" as a Style

I'd grown up as a fan of University of Michigan basketball—my family decided they were Michigan fans, and by default, that was the chosen team of my youth. The connection was bolstered by the presence of Michigan's Fab Five—Chris Webber, Jalen Rose, Juwan Howard, Jimmy King, and Ray Jackson—in the early 1990s.

They played flashy, they dressed flashy, they pissed off old white people in the suburb I grew up in. They were perfect for a young teenager who was struggling to buy into the longstanding puritanical view of sports, that they represented some sort of moralistic environment where sportsmanship, humility, and effort epitomized value. I just wanted some dunks, and the Fab Five delivered.

But by the end of the 1990s as I was maturing (slightly), forced to work to have any sort of independence, and preparing to enter and try to pay my own way through college, my allegiance suddenly and permanently switched to Michigan State with the arrival of four players who had grown up a short distance from where I did.

I was ready for substance over style, and four teenagers went to Michigan State University in the late 1990s confident in one thing—the city they grew up in prepared them with a toughness that uniquely positioned them for success.

By the year 2000, they'd led Michigan State to a NCAA championship and, quite intentionally, thrust Flint into the national spotlight. Mateen Cleaves, Morris Peterson, Charlie Bell, and Antonio Smith (who graduated in 1999, prior to the team's championship breakthrough) became synonymous with their hometown—even successfully appropriating the Flintstones name from Hanna-Barbera and giving it a new, gritty identity.

Flint Northern's Smith, despite being undersized among opposing frontcourt peers, was equipped with a stoic toughness, a willingness to engage in battles with bigger brutes under the basket, and an impressive ability to infuse that fearlessness onto his teammates. He became the big man by which all other future Tom Iz-zo-coached big men would be measured in terms of heart and toughness.

Peterson was an under-recruited wing from Flint Northwestern who developed a jack-of-all-trades skill set that made him a first-round pick in the NBA draft and a mainstay in NBA rotations for nearly a decade.

Bell, whose scoring ability at Flint Southwestern attracted crowds from around the state to watch him play, molded himself into a serviceable defensive player and a versatile playmaker capable of creating shots for others.

Flint Northern's Cleaves—the team's point guard, star player, and unquestioned on-court leader—played in the 2000 National Championship game on a badly injured ankle, and highlights of him hobbling around the court are still played every March during the NCAA Tournament.

Collectively, they were resilient, rebounding from a loss in the Final Four in 1999 before their breakthrough the following season. They worked and improved throughout their college careers. Although all four were good high school players, only Cleaves was recruited as a can't-miss star prospect. And they took very seriously their place as stewards of Flint's vast basketball tradition, building on what their predecessors accomplished and raising the bar for future generations.

The group famously sported "Flint'" tattoos—not just meant as a narcissistic homage to the city. Cleaves once told me, "There's something that comes behind that tattoo—it's about work, it's grind, it's dedication. It's not fun."[8]

And, unsurprisingly, their statement resonated with players who grew up watching and idolizing them. "I don't think there's a basketball player in Flint who doesn't have that tattoo now," Bell joked in an interview in 2010.[9]

The environment the Flintstones grew up in—with Division I-caliber prospects leading each high school team in the city—no longer exists, but the ethos and culture they contributed to will always resonate as a deep source of pride.

Much like the Fab Five, the Flintstones carved out a national niche as an iconic, nicknamed unit that will forever be imprinted on the history of college basketball. They did it by converting grittiness, toughness, and, most importantly, Flint, into an identity every bit as charismatic as the "flash" peddled by the Fab Five.

---

8   Hayes, Patrick. "10 years after winning the national title, 'The Flintstones' are still making an impact on the Flint community." *Flint Journal*, March 19, 2010. Accessed: http://blog.mlive.com/flintjournal/hotbed-hoops/2010/03/10_years_after_winning_the_national_title_the_flin.html

9   Ibid

Merging Rivals—A Painful Necessity

During the 1980s, the Flint Central basketball team had such an embarrassingly abundant supply of talent that legendary coach Stan Gooch has an interesting claim to fame among his many accomplishments: he once cut a future NBA All-Star.

Latrell Sprewell had a standout NBA career, including All-Star appearances and league awards, but he is a name never mentioned among Flint basketball greats. And it's because he never actually played in Flint despite living in the city as a teenager.

Sprewell tried out for the varsity team at Flint Central as a freshman and was cut by Gooch after his first practice. Sprewell then moved to Milwaukee, where he became a high school star, was an eventual first round pick in the NBA Draft and had a lengthy and … memorable[10] professional career.

As insane as it sounds, Gooch was probably justified in cutting Sprewell. At the time, Flint Central was the standard in high school basketball in the state of Michigan. Central won three consecutive state championships in the early 1980s.

By the 1990s, though, the city's dominant basketball program had become Flint Northern, led by Cleaves and Smith. Northern won a state championship in 1995.

The two schools had a heated and competitive rivalry that extended over multiple decades and wasn't limited to just basketball—the annual Thanksgiving Day football game between Northern and Central at Atwood Stadium frequently drew approximately 10,000 spectators.

Combining the talent of both schools would've resulted in an embarrassment of athletic riches, creating a dynastic and unbeatable high school powerhouse—there are some potential 1980s Central/Northwestern lineups that would've run major college teams out of the gym.

In 2009, that outlandish concept became a reality when Flint Central closed and four players who would've been seniors at Central transferred to Northern.

Early in that season, the coaching staff at Northern invited Mateen Cleaves to speak to the team and reiterate the legacy the players were now a part of.

Cleaves, never shy about publicly calling attention to causes he believed in, showed up promoting his latest cause—former Michigan State wide receiver Plaxico Burress. Burress, then a star player for the New York Giants, accidentally shot himself at a club in 2008 and was subsequently convicted under New York's strict

10   Puma, Mike. "The 'Choke' Artist." ESPN.com, December 1, 1997. Accessed: http://espn.go.com/classic/s/add_sprewell_latrell.html

gun laws and sentenced to two years in prison.[11] Cleaves was protesting the admittedly harsh sentence in T-shirt form—"Free Plax'" emblazoned on the front, and "Bloomberg" with a slash through it on the back.

The team was attentive, and despite the more than ten years since Cleaves had played in that gym, the players were deferential to his accomplishments and receptive to his message—mainly, that there was an expectation associated with playing at Flint Northern that the team would contend for championships.

Cleaves noted that the team had quite a lengthy state title drought. "It's a shame that the last banner up on that wall is from when I was here in 1995," Cleaves told them.[12]

Cleaves' message was well-intentioned—he and many other former Flint players regularly spend time with young people and encourage them. But the expectation that players in this generation have the resources to accomplish what those in previous generations did is misguided; no amount of individual work by the players Cleaves was addressing would've changed their ceiling as a team.

The merger didn't result in a state title contender, or even a feel-good story about players from both schools merging together seamlessly and having a strong season. The Vikings had no perimeter shooting, making it difficult for the team's two best players, Shaquille Smith and Gerald Williams-Taylor, to use their best skills, slashing to the basket. Defenses, not scared by any of the team's perimeter threats, routinely packed players inside, resulting in some awful shooting games and pedestrian results for the season. Northern finished in the middle of the pack in its conference and couldn't even get out of its district in the playoffs, let alone make a championship run. And, embarrassingly, in a game against Detroit Country Day, Northern resorted to holding the ball for long periods of time just past the halfcourt line in an effort to shorten the game. This is often a strategy employed by outmatched rural or suburban high school teams against stronger city teams to limit the number of possessions by more talented squads and keep the game closer. To see a Flint team do this against a good-but-not-great Country Day team was embarrassing—angry

11   "Burress begins sentence in gun case." ESPN.com, September 23, 2009. Accessed: http://espn.go.com/nfl/news/story?id=4493887

12   Hayes, Patrick. "Mateen Cleaves talks to Flint Northern basketball team about tradition." *Flint Journal*, December 11, 2009. Accessed: http://blog.mlive.com/flintjournal/hotbedhoops/2009/12/mateen_cleaves_talks_to_flint_northern_basketball.html

murmurs and shouts of "COME ON, TUCK!" at then-Northern coach Thomas Tucker were clearly audible.

A few years later, in 2013, Northern would also close, bringing to an end two of the city's incredible basketball legacies in less than five years.

The Fabulist

The emails started in 2009, as soon as a few of my bylines covering high school basketball appeared in the *Flint Journal*. There were at least three different names, all very common, but the only one I remember is "Thomas Smith." The content of their messages was the same, with suspiciously similar phrasing and terminology used by these "different people." And the message was clear: I needed to check out a kid named Roy Jackson at Hamady High School, a small district on the outskirts of the city limits.

Despite warnings from colleagues, who had all been targeted by the same email campaigns and had learned to ignore them, I was willing to put aside the fact that I was clearly being played and see for myself. I drove to the tiny Hamady gym — think of a typical resource-strapped inner-city high school, only about a quarter the size, and that's Hamady, located just outside of Flint but close enough for residents to share the same pride of growing up in a tough, hardknock community.

I watched Roy play, and saw a solid high school player who had a work ethic that his coach routinely praised. He was clearly good enough to play low-level college basketball somewhere. That's a great accomplishment — few high school players are good enough to play college basketball at any level.

But Jackson was also a player whose dreams outweighed his potential. That's also not uncommon — most anyone who plays organized sports has high hopes for professional success. As a fifteen-year-old in 1997, practicing alone on my grandparents' farm in Lapeer, Michigan, my dream was completely laid out. I'd become a high school star at Lapeer West High School, skip college, and enter the 1999 NBA draft upon graduation, win Rookie of the Year with the Detroit Pistons, be chosen to play on the 2000 United States Olympic Basketball team, meet U.S. gymnast Dominique Moceanu, fall in love and get married, then go on to a prolific NBA career as a deadly perimeter sharpshooter. I was Steph Curry before there was a Steph Curry. (Dominique and I probably would've had kids who are adorbs and our own cooking show, just like Steph and Ayesha Curry, too.)

Anyway, the point is, I could relate to Roy and his dreams. Industrious as he was about his college prospects, Roy would not be deterred by reality, and with his army of email accounts, photos of stationery from high major Division I colleges with his name on it, and even stories of recruiting visits to those campuses (hey, a visit to Duke is still a visit to Duke, even if Coach K doesn't invite you), he was prepared to try and convince anyone who would listen of his abundant options.

When his Division I plans didn't work out directly out of high school, he landed an opportunity at a community college and did well enough to earn the chance to finish his eligibility playing low-level college basketball if he wanted to. Instead, his admirable propaganda campaign continued—the high major offers were once again pouring in and he was once again touring the country looking for the right university to serve as the springboard to his NBA career. His final choice wasn't Duke or North Carolina or Wake Forest or any of the other potential suitors his mysterious email supporters had predicted—it was tiny Arkansas Pine-Bluff.

He appeared in five games during his lone season of Division I college basketball, scoring five total points.

He did not play his senior season, briefly appeared in lower rung "professional" leagues—the type of leagues famous mainly for not paying their players—and, a full two years after appearing in a college game, filled out the paperwork to make himself eligible for the 2016 NBA draft.

Along the way, he constructed an impressive social media presence that included professional-quality selfies, inspirational quotes about his NBA pursuit, and comparisons of himself to some of basketball's biggest stars. The entertainingly boastful and completely lacking in self-awareness social media campaign, incidentally, stood in stark contrast to his humble and soft-spoken personality in face-to-face interviews.

Jackson won't ever play in the NBA, and there's nothing wrong with that. But too often, kids grow up fixated on a dream that is only reachable for a few, poorly advised by adults who don't know any better, fruitlessly pursue it, and—in the process—ignore the other avenues to create successful lives for themselves, most notably missing opportunities for a free education.

The athletic tradition in Flint creates an impression that there's only one way to escape the immense burdens of living in the inner city, resulting in a singular focus in kids who don't have the talent to achieve those heights, but can't imagine themselves doing anything else.

The fact is, Roy was trying to work me, and tried to work multiple other sports reporters to gain publicity, which he thought would help him achieve his dreams. But rather than get upset about it, it produced in me an eye-opening epiphany about the symbiotically exploitative relationship between athletes and the media.

Jackson wasn't a star athletic prospect. If he was, news outlets would've undoubtedly devoted resources to covering him. That coverage wouldn't result from some warm-hearted mission to cover the most newsworthy stories. It would've resulted from the fact that star athletes help media outlets attract eyeballs to their online products, sell print products, and even develop new products—hello, poster inserts and photo prints that can be ordered!—to sell. I had no problem with Roy trying to take advantage of a system that by its very nature sets out to profit from the accomplishments of others.

The City Gives and Takes

At its best, the gritty, blue-collar toughness the city is known for creates athletes infused with the self-assuredness that they can overcome any challenge presented by the sports world after dealing with the real-world struggles that accompany day-to-day living in the most downtrodden regions of Flint.

At its worst, the dangers of growing up in an area plagued by violence, crime, and poverty aren't picky about where they manifest themselves.

Former Flint Northwestern star Jody Allen was murdered.[13] Former Flint Central star Takais Brown was charged with robbing and murdering a seventy-nine-year-old.[14] After his best NBA season, drugs were discovered in Terry Furlow's system after his fatal car accident.[15]

In 2016, Cleaves—long looked at as a golden child of Flint for his charitable work in the community and squeaky clean image—was charged with sexual assault after allegedly taking a twenty-four-year-old woman to a motel, holding her against her will, and sexually assaulting her, according to prosecutors.

Growing up surrounded by rampant poverty, crime, drugs, and other forms of loveless and lawless behavior have often proven to be character-shaping for people

13   Woodyard, Eric. "Jody Allen's death shock community." *Flint Journal*, July 16, 2012. Accessed: http://www.mlive.com/sports/flint/index.ssf/2012/07/jody_allens_death_shocks_commu.html

14   Woodyard, Eric. "Takais Brown, one of three charged with murder, known around Flint for shooting hoops, not guns." *Flint Journal*, August 14, 2014. Accessed: http://www.mlive.com/sports/flint/index.ssf/2014/08/takais_brown.html

15   Woodyard, Eric. "Original Old School: Gone Too Soon." *SLAM*, June 20, 2010. Accessed: http://www.slamonline.com/nba/original-old-school-gone-too-soon/#RVSdl55u5clFjkSf.97

who overcome that environment and achieve success. However, the violent surroundings, combined with the culture of privilege and unaccountabililty that sports
stardom in any environment can foster, have also been the downfall of many.

After a 2008-09 season filled with mediocre play by all city teams, Flint Northwestern gave the greatest hope that I would get to cover a throwback, dominant team
in 2009-10. They were the best team in the city the previous season, returned four
starters, including their three leading scorers, and added a high-scoring transfer
from Hamady High School in Dominez Burnett.

They were a team with four players who had legitimate chances to play college
basketball and were great high school players, plus a collection of role players who
complemented the skills of their stars well.

They were also the team I'd covered the most in 2008-09, and I'd formed what
I considered good relationships with many players on the team. I'd run into some
of them around town and they'd talk to me. I'd met some of their moms and would
make small talk with them in the stands during games. I started off on the beat with
no connections and, by the end of one season, felt confident that I was gaining trust
and becoming a part of the Flint basketball world that I found so intriguing.

But, not only would those assumptions be shaken, the Flint Northwestern basketball team would become a painful example of the tragic consequences of poor
decisions.

In August of 2009, Willis "Ray" Arrington, a starting forward on the team and
a star wide receiver on the football team, was shot and killed. Arrington and five
others were reportedly attempting to break into a house when the homeowner shot
at them.[16]

Dominez Burnett was arrested and charged with armed robbery in early 2011.[17]

For a reporter who covered those players and got to know them on some basic
level, these incidents were a painful reminder that I was still an outsider. I had
no comprehension of who they were outside of the basketball context I saw them
in. I had no way of understanding the day-to-day stress of living in a crime-filled

16   Hayes, Patrick. "Flint basketball community coping with the death of talented and well-liked Flint North-
      western athlete Willis Arrington." *Flint Journal*, August 20, 2010. Accessed: http://highschoolsports.mlive.
      com/news/article/-1424376069459948227/flint-basketball-community-coping-with-the-death-of-talented-
      and-well-liked-flint-northwestern-athlete-willis-arrington/

17   Dougovito, Lori. "Northwestern High School senior faces charges." ABC 12, January 18, 2011. Accessed:
      http://abc7.com/archive/7905169/

environment surrounded by people who make decisions without their best interest at heart or, in some cases, with downright malicious intentions.

When Arrington was killed, I was lost in terms of how to cover the story. On the one hand, he was a likable, polite kid who I'd gotten to know a bit through interactions with him and his teammates over the course of approximately a year, and I felt a strong need to honor that. On the other, there's no way to justify what he was doing at the time he was killed, and I in no way wanted to minimize that.

The indecision paralyzed me temporarily. Thankfully, I wasn't left alone with my thoughts long. Mike Williams, a great basketball coach at Beecher High School, located just outside the city limits, a teacher at Flint Northwestern, and one of the few adults involved in coaching who I'd comfortably call a mentor to the kids he interacted with, called me before I'd even formulated a plan to run by an editor.

"I just wanted to say some good words about Ray," Williams told me, before poignantly and painfully discussing the many warnings he'd given Arrington and other students he taught and coached in Flint—including a story about a friend he had growing up who was killed in a similar attempted robbery.

The violence, the crime, the lack of attention and supervision, and the lack of access to necessary resources are recurring problems in Flint and cities like it all over the country. They're problems that coaches like Williams are forced to cope with—the supervision, safety, and guidance you can provide to students is limited to hours in school or the gym for practice and games. What do you do when the kids go home?

And yet …

Despite the turmoil surrounding that Northwestern team, despite the tragedies they experienced together, there were two incredible success stories that played out years later.

Deondre Parks, a sharpshooting guard who a teacher at Northwestern once told me was given waivers to continue playing even when he should've been academically ineligible, didn't graduate high school on time. That's not an unfamiliar story in Flint. The district's graduation rate is approximately sixty percent, and the dropout rate is above twenty percent.[18]

Except Parks' story took a sharp twist there. He attended prep schools in Missis-

---

18   MI Schools Data, Accessed: https://www.mischooldata.org/DistrictSchoolProfiles/StudentInformation/
GraduationDropoutRate.aspx

sippi and then Georgia in order to graduate high school, then played junior college basketball in Iowa.[19] He performed well enough to earn a scholarship to Division I South Dakota State University, and in 2016, he led SDSU to the NCAA Tournament as one of the team's top players.

His performance there positioned him for not only a potential professional career somewhere, but more importantly, an opportunity to graduate from college. For reference, only about eleven percent of Flint residents have a bachelor's degree according to U.S. Census data.

Parks' former teammate, Burnett, has an equally inspiring—and improbable, given the odds—story. Burnett missed his senior season at Northwestern after being charged with armed robbery. He later accepted a plea agreement and ended up at a prep school in East Lansing, Michigan.

A versatile, lanky and high-scoring prospect in high school, Burnett saw virtually all of his college opportunities disappear after his legal issues. Davenport University, a NAIA school in Grand Rapids, remained interested, however, and Burnett signed there after finishing high school.

He wrapped up an incredible four-year college career in 2016, winning consecutive NAIA National Player of the Year awards his junior and senior seasons. Burnett also has a unique claim to fame—with more than 2,700 career points, he's the state of Michigan's all-time leading scorer at any level of college basketball.[20]

He positioned himself for a potential professional basketball career, and also became a star in the classroom—making the Dean's List at Davenport.

For those who succeed, the struggles of life in Flint are the foundation of a positive narrative for overcoming obstacles. But for far more people those struggles create a reality that is often inescapable.

For decades, Flint has faced a seemingly endless—and escalating in magnitude—series of crises that would cause a weaker city to crumble. And yet the city is the birthplace of the American auto industry, and Flint has produced a litany of talented innovators, artists, entertainers, thinkers, and athletes. There's a nuanced

19   Zimmer, Mike. "Deondre Parks: Hero at Home." *Argus Leader*, March 3, 2016. Accessed: http://www.argusleader.com/story/sports/college/south-dakota-state-university/2016/03/03/hero-home/81237716/

20   Woodyard, Eric. "Flint's Dominez Burnett wins national player of the year again." *Flint Journal*, March 17, 2016. Accessed: http://www.mlive.com/sports/flint/index.ssf/2016/03/flints_dominez_burnett_named_n.html

history here that has made vital contributions to the development of the United States.

Basketball is a perfect example of precisely why Flint endures. Watching a high school basketball game in a musty gym in Flint, it's impossible to not feel a part of something important. Regardless of who is on the court, of who is coaching the teams, of who is sitting at the scorer's table writing about the game, of who is watching in the stands … there's a sense of responsibility to live up to and honor the standards created by the success of predecessors in those gyms.

In recent years, as the quality of Flint basketball has decreased, there has been no shortage of critics who willingly–and sometimes gleefully–point out the short-comings of the latest generation of athletes. But the experiences of those kids, the struggles they have, the hopes they have, and the very real sense of pride they take in being able to call themselves a part of Flint's basketball legacy are all as present as they ever were. The city's circumstances have deteriorated immensely since the peaks of basketball dominance the city once enjoyed, but the atmosphere in the city's basketball landscape endures through all.

Flint is the best basketball city in America. Try and tell us otherwise.

Flint Out Loud

TRACI CURRIE

Out of the night that covers me,
  Black as the Pit from pole to pole,
I thank whatever gods may be
  For my unconquerable soul.

In the fell clutch of circumstance
  I have not winced nor cried aloud.
Under the bludgeonings of chance
  My head is bloody, but unbowed.

Beyond this place of wrath and tears
  Looms but the Horror of the shade,
And yet the menace of the years
  Finds, and shall find, me unafraid.

It matters not how strait the gate,
  How charged with punishments the scroll,
I am the master of my fate:
  I am the captain of my soul.

  – *"Invictus", by William Ernest Henley*

In 2004 I decided to relocate to Flint, Michigan, from Ohio. Right before I moved, my family asked me, "Are you sure about moving there?" The question they were actually asking was, "Do you know where you are moving to, because I do (according to Wikipedia and a few news clippings)." I had researched the university location and the teaching position I was interviewing for, but I didn't know Flint. I would argue that you never really know a place until you settle in.

Now, when reflecting on my life in Flint, I have to ask myself, "When did I actually settle in?" And truth be told, although I tell people I am a part of Flint, I am a resident of Flint, on some days I am Flint, I have questioned whether or not Flint and I mesh. We talk to each other, especially in the early mornings when I need to commune with nature. We hang out like friends do (before the sun sets, that is), but "settling in" is a funny phrase to claim in this Midwest city people call a Li'l Detroit or GM town or dangerous city or, most recently, poisonous brown urban sprawl. Interestingly enough, it is not completely brown: fifty-six percent Black, thirty-seven percent White, three percent Hispanic, and three percent other races. Sometimes I hate statistics. Don't you?

As a residential tourist I was in search of a literary arts scene when I first moved here. I needed to engage with other performance poets. I worked in Flint and was a part of the academic scene, but I spent most of my time in Detroit, because that's where the art took me. Detroit felt like home because spoken word artists welcomed me into their spaces with open arms and showed me that performance poetry was another form of art therapy. Three years later I created and taught a spoken word course at the University of Michigan-Flint. It was experimental and exciting. For the first time I started to feel as if Flint was a viable space for change, because I was teaching a subject that informed who I was as an artist and educator. In other words, I created my artistic niche in Flint.

I spent less time in Detroit and more time in Flint. Later a friend and I created a monthly spoken word series that featured performance artists as well as an open mic for writers and poets. I was at the height of my game in this city. I felt as if I was giving something back to Flint.

A few years later, in 2011, I was asked to create a performance arts program at Genesee Valley Regional Center (GVRC), a juvenile detention center on Pasadena Avenue. The purpose of the program is to artistically work with youth between the ages of ten and seventeen who have found themselves in a quandary. Some people might call this quandary a state of volatility. The young women I work with have NOT experienced the American apple pie dream. Let's just call some of their experiences a nightmare. My job is to step into GVRC and create a safe space for literary and oral expression. Their job is to write their stories down and, in time, say them right out loud. Ultimately, myself and Jade, the other co-facilitator, are building confidence and self-esteem; we are sharpening their life skills; we are helping the young women communicate more effectively, especially when they are called to address the judge in court. We are not saviors. We are facilitators and supporters in this process of cultivation.

I could go anywhere in the world and do this sort of work, right? Wrong. I was approached in Flint, not Ohio or Delaware (where I grew up) or North Carolina (another one of my stomping grounds). I wanted to identify myself with spoken word in Flint for a few reasons. For one, spoken word is performance poetry for the stage. That stage has different appearances—it can be the courtroom in front of the judge or a classroom setting in front of one's peers. It can be around the kitchen table when an argument is about to ensue and words must be chosen carefully. One of my greatest examples occurred this past February. When I was in the detention center, one of the young women who had been in and out of the center several times over the past year was expressing how frustrated she was because she felt alone. On this particular evening she wrote about her mother's lack of response to her phone calls:

Why have you abandoned me?
What have I done to you?
I thought you loved me?
I thought I was your child.
I understand that I'm not the best child to have
But you told me you did what you did because God said.
He brought you to my rescue
But now that I am older
you have abandoned me and left me
out in the cold. I wish I could understand but
you won't answer my calls or talk to me but
deep down inside I truly love you and I have not
abandoned you or forgotten you at all. I wish you
would do the same with me.

My job was to encourage her to write. Just write. There was no need for me to offer any solutions, because she already knows the solutions. She is one of the sharpest young women I know. She instructs other young women around her to make better decisions. It's funny how easy it is to give advice but difficult to take one's own advice. She admitted this. She knows it's hard outside of GVRC. These stories are why I show up to the center. Spoken word at its best right here in Flint!

Relationships are occurring in these spaces simply because I show up and activate my senses—sight, hearing, and sometimes a necessary hug. The stories are endless. Some of the young women have entered abusive spaces where they have been ignored mentally, emotionally, and physically. Some have turned to self-harm as a coping mechanism. Some are willing to sacrifice their lives for their siblings or their own children. Yes, some of the women are parents. Some profess their undying love for God while others question God.

When I reflect on my Flint journey, I realize that spoken word has always been an avenue to create a space for my existence. If I was going to stay in this city, I had to have a reason to stay. Teaching four classes every semester was not enough. I needed to feel like the tides were changing in the faces I saw. I didn't want to just teach classes that are required for students. I wanted people to choose spoken word as their lifeline just because they could.

When I and my co-facilitator enter a space, we begin with naming oneself. We must name ourselves as a reminder that no one will overtake our beings. Those are the evenings we become William Ernest Henley's "Invictus". And after naming who and what we are in that GVRC spoken word space, the girls speak. They share their truths. They hear their own voices ring aloud and click to their own time; and hands rise with urgency as if no one has allowed some of them to speak their worst pain and joyful moments. They transition their stories from air to paper so they can map their thoughts—their stories, their pain, themselves—in whatever form necessary: pictures, words, doodling, and however else those words just spoken fall onto the page.

Feeling a Little Subprime

TEDDY ROBERTSON

Note: An earlier version of this essay appeared
online in East Village Magazine.

A fter the financial crisis of 2008 and the revelation that subprime mortgages
were involved in the bubble that had burst, commentators intoned that we'd
just gone too far in America with everyone wanting to own their own home. This
folly was attributed to (among others) George W. Bush. When he came into office
in 2002 he promoted an "ownership society," in which owning a home would give
people a stake in society. Attractive to voters and lucrative for Wall Street under lax
regulation—a "win-win" vision.

Then, lo! The crash of global banks, the faltering of the credit market, and the
near collapse of finance. Exposed underneath it all were mortgage-backed securi-
ties: tranches of mortgages, bundles of bad loans to eager new buyers unqualified
for a "conventional" loan, buyers with low credit scores, nothing in the bank for a
down payment, and one paycheck away from default. The shady subprime world
was revealed.

I've followed this drama; it's infinitely complex, riddled with arcane phrases and
acronyms, packed with factors besides bad mortgages. Nothing rivets me to the TV
screen like an interview with economists like Joseph Stiglitz or Paul Krugman. Or
better yet, someone I can understand, like Sheila Bair. And don't get me started on
the movies: *Too Big to Fail, Margin Call, Inside Job, The Big Short.*

I have a stake in this topic because I own a house that I love more than it's
worth. My love has grown as its market value has declined. It's a healthy house
from head to toe—with a new roof and a dry basement. Large windows face the
sunrise. In its backyard I grow roses that bloom from June to November.

And the house has a congenial setting—a neighborhood.

I'm new to the neighborhood idea. As a kid I lived on the hillsides of northern

California. Only a few houses were visible; it was an "unincorporated area," outside
the city limits. Nobody lived "next door." We had fields and scrub brush, septic
tanks, dirt and gravel roads, and sometimes, in the summer, a random rattlesnake
that got killed with a shovel. When you saw a neighbor, it was thanks to an emergency—for example, a finger severed with a scythe.

As an adult, I lived in a big city, on the top floor of a high-rise apartment building. I learned the nuances of nods and mumbles, the social norms of the elevator
and the hallway. After that, I lived in a small town on Main Street. Everyone
minded their own business, knew what you bought at the IGA, observed what you
wore to church, and commented on how you raised your kid. It was ingrown and
insufferable.

So when I came to live in Flint, and bought a house in a part of the city called
Mott Park, I didn't understand the real value of a neighborhood—until the mortgage
crisis of 2008.

Mott Park developed from a housing vision that preceded former President
Bush by at least three decades. In 1919 General Motors created a subsidiary called
the Modern Housing Corporation to build a residential area of sturdy, affordable
houses. It was GM's response to the needs of auto workers in Flint, Pontiac, and
Detroit: a planned neighborhood. The first Mott Park homes were built in 1921;
the area filled in street by street. By 1933, private developers built Mott Park's
remaining homes, including those along Nolen Drive like mine. Larger and more
architecturally complex, these houses sit on lots along the Flint River across from a
city golf course. Varied building styles, curvilinear streets, a public park, and many
trees made the neighborhood attractive. Mott Park exemplified an American dream
accessible to the working class.

Photos and reminiscences document this neighborhood in its mid-twentieth-cen-
tury heyday. *The Mott Park Chronicles*, compiled by two local residents, shows
happy 1950s families, children on the sidewalks heading off to nearby schools.[1]
There'd be family car in the driveway (probably a Buick). It was a lifestyle of pride
in home ownership that lasted several decades, precisely the years of President
Bush's youth.The 50s afterglow was still warm when I bought a house in the neighborhood in 1995, even though Flint had suffered in the decades-long decline of the
auto industry. Since the 2008 mortgage and financial crisis, the "great recession,"
sharper signs of hardship mingle with new values and new ways.

---

1   Cathy Snyder, ed. *Mott Park Chronicles. The Story of an American Neighborhood: Historic Photos &
    Memories of Life in Flint, Michigan, 1908-2009* (Grand Blanc, MI: Grand Blanc Printing Company, 2009).

Homeowners who could afford to leave the neighborhood have moved away. Some left for typical reasons. Older folks retired; the dogs they used to walk have died. Younger couples want better schools or more bedrooms as the kids grow up. Others have left because of issues with crime and a decline in safety enforcement. And still others were unable to keep their homes; they lost a job and could not re-finance. Some were subprime buyers with no options, so they just decamped, increasing the number of vacant homes. One week all seems normal; the next, people are just gone and the house is suddenly empty. Through the glass of uncovered windows, rooms at the back of the house are visible. How long did these people deliberate before slipping away? Their months of desperation were not visible to the Sunday walker.

Meantime, banks try to recoup something; investment companies buy up bundles of properties. In Flint in 2008, fifty-three percent of homes were owned by investment companies, twenty-nine percent were real-estate owned, and sixteen percent were privately owned. Of those investors, twenty-two percent were out-of-state companies, twenty-one percent located in Michigan, twenty-seven percent in Genesee County, twenty-three percent in Flint, and six percent in Mott Park itself.[2]

Fewer traditional property owners live here now. The newcomers live in a different world than those for whom these houses were built or the first generation of homeowners that followed them. Renters, lease-holders, welfare agency clients — they too surely enjoy the freedom, fresh air, and green expanses that still-decent houses in a fairly good neighborhood provide. But what former apartment dweller moves in with a lawnmower? The yard around the house or the paint and repairs are probably not the renters' responsibility; landlords do the minimum, usually less. If people are buying on land contract, they can make payments, but not much more.

My unscientific calculation is that a single-family dwelling occupied by renters can last about two years before external decline sets in. A vacant house goes in a year. Some edges of the Mott Park neighborhood have gone beyond reclaiming. A Genesee County Land Bank assessment charts the changing status of the neighborhood's housing stock. A color-coded map of parcels rates the houses as good (rose), fair (pink), poor (violet), or structurally deficient (red).[3] You can see which proper-

---

2   Vacant Properties Survey; June – August 2008; City of Flint Assessor's Web site (August 31, 2008), as cited in Susan Burhans, "Mott Park Neighborhood Stabilization Plan" [working document], October 2, 2012.

3   Genesee County Land Bank, Mott Park Housing Condition Assessment 2012, Nov. 7, 2012.

ties the Land Bank owns and where the tax foreclosures are.[4]

I'm over the shock of the changes, visual ones mostly, and even the drastic loss of property value. I've discovered something else that seems to matter now and it's tied to the neighborhood, a bunch of people all in the same rickety residential lifeboat. They have grit, like the autoworkers who first lived in Mott Park. Neighborhood residents raise money to repair the playground. They patch the asphalt on the tennis courts, hang new nets, and repair fencing. A small grant enables gardeners to plant the public flower beds laid out a half-century ago. Volunteers adopt a street to keep free of trash. Twice a year student volunteers from Kettering University and nearby churches join in to clear blighted streets and alleys. Residents constructed four little libraries for kids in the neighborhood and joined the movement of "Little Free Libraries." When the city abandoned the golf course, a neighborhood group organized to ensure that the land is mowed and to solicit ideas to develop it for year-round recreation.

The Facebook pages that hold some of these efforts together show how creative, energetic, and diverse these neighborhood people are. Neighborhood meetings can be volatile as residents with little shared background or history struggle to make decisions together. Stakes are high when you have nowhere else to go.

I drive through other distinctive neighborhoods in Flint like College and Cultural Center or Woodcroft, areas with larger and more imposing homes, that were built in the 1920s for scions of the auto industry or company managers. I'm amazed at how solid they still seem, with their slate roofs and horseshoe drives. The telltale signs are less visible in these areas that suffered less in the decades of automotive collapse that weakened Flint before 2008. My eye is canny, however; I know how much change can be hidden. Friends in those neighborhoods worry too; they are often reluctant to speak, lest they contribute to the perceived devaluation of their investment.

As for Mott Park, the year 2019 marks the centennial of its founding, of a historic relationship between America's workers and the automotive industry in the city of Flint. Most of the plants are gone now and the number of remaining workers is a fraction of what it once was. But much of their housing survives. And the people in those homes are not subprime at all.

---

4   The Land Bank owns five properties in Mott Park: two have been completed rehabbed; two have rehab in progress, and one is a pending sale. Buyers just need to qualify for a mortgage. The payments are cheaper than rent. See http://www.thelandbank.org/ Accessed November 2, 2012. The Land Bank was established in 2002 after a 1999 Michigan tax law change.

2302 Welch

WILL CRONIN

The day I came home from the hospital, my dad, so the story goes, carried me first to the front door of our house and then all around the outside, whispering in my ear, "This is where you live. This is your house." Then he walked me through the inside and repeated the same mantra. That was thirty-two years ago.

I spent a long time with mixed feelings about that house. I would occasionally visit schoolmates' houses—especially starting in middle school when I left the Flint public schools and went off to what passes for a snooty private school in Genesee County—and their palatial abodes in the woods of Holly and on the arboreal lanes of Flushing and edging the pontoon-boat-bedecked shores of Lake Fenton made my little house in Flint feel like something akin to a Quonset hut set in the atomic wasteland of some benighted atoll in the middle of the Pacific.

"You mean you can walk all the way to the park? And up to 7-11? Alone?"

After my dad died in the early 1990s, my mom considered moving us out. In hindsight, we surely could have done it. We had my dad's UAW/GM pension and Social Security. We could have moved down to an apartment in Grand Blanc, a small city south of the Flint where my grandmother lived, or maybe bought a little five-room house on some dirt side street on the edge of a suburb, Davison maybe. It would not have been any great shakes, but at least we could have put out jack-o'-lanterns at Halloween without them getting smashed and I could have, perhaps, had a bike that didn't get stolen.

I love trains. The Christmas after my father died, in an effort to bring some cheer to a time of deep despair, Mom came home with a little Christmas train decoration, an engine and three or four little train cars covered in lights. We put it up outside under the front window. It was destroyed that same night. The next morning, we looked at the little tangled pile of broken plastic, wire, and glass, and we never tried to decorate again. Life retreated inside, and remained there.

We stayed. The reality was my mom was not in any condition to undertake a move like that then. We had a house, it was paid for, it was sound. And we stayed. We stayed through our car being stolen from our driveway, we stayed through our garage and shed being broken into numerous times (curiously, no one ever actually came in the house), we stayed through our neighbors across the street barely surviving an armed home invasion that left a spray of birdshot in the siding next to their door. Lying on the living room floor until one in the morning was an annual New Year's morning tradition, as the gunfire outside pop-pop-poppity-pop-popped away.

I no longer lived there permanently when I went off to college in 2000, but my mom remained. I worried about her; she was a single older woman in a neighborhood that was truly dangerous. But by that time, we didn't really have options. When I turned eighteen, the Social Security went away and we were stuck. I moved around after college to work in Washington, D.C. and to graduate school in Grand Rapids, on the prosperous west side of Michigan. My mom was always in Flint, and when I had days off, I was always there, too. Strangely, the horror of the 1990s seemed to subside as the 2000s wore on. The neighborhood quieted down. It felt safer. We reclaimed our backyard, scraping the accumulated mud off the patio and washing down the deck. The scrubby trees and bushes we'd let grow up around the house came down. The old brick barbeque in the corner of the yard, a ruin entangled in brambles for my entire life, was cleaned up and became a modest fire pit.

My friends and I grew up, and weekends were spent downtown hoisting an elbow and discoursing on world events at the Torch Bar & Grill and the Soggy Bottom Bar and the White Horse Tavern, Flint institutions where young, idealistic transplants rub elbows with grizzled political bosses and regulars of longstanding. Mom and my aunt emptied out the upstairs a bit, and the bedroom up there became the "love nest," as my aunt called it, where my girlfriend, now my wife, and I would sleep when we came to visit. Slowly the little house on Welch and Seneca began to feel like home again.

The late 2000s were the most optimistic time in Flint that I can remember. Downtown was on a slow but steady path back to relevance. People were living there. People were working there. It was the best place north of Detroit and east of Grand Rapids to have a night out with friends. It seemed like there were big ideas bubbling everywhere. We talked on and on about urban farming and adaptive reuse over craft pale ale and complementary Torch popcorn. There are so many great buildings there, with great bones, we said. There are so many schools. There are so many smart, young, motivated people here. The wind is blowing our way.

I was a believer. I was in graduate school in urban planning, and I desperately wanted to be a part of it. I wanted to help my hometown, where the American Dream, such as it ever was, if it ever was, burned brightest and hottest. Where we, if only for an instant and only if you looked in the right place, could see the future that could have been, where everyone might have had it okay.

But reality intruded. I was a newly minted planner looking for a job in a place where everyone, it seemed, was a planner, and there were no planning jobs anyway. It was not to be. I found work in my field elsewhere, in exile in Wisconsin. The break had come. I was leaving now for good and that meant my mom could not stay either. The cracks were beginning to show in the optimism of the late 2000s. The houses in our neighborhood were emptying faster now, and being gutted just as quickly. Even as my friends and I partied away the weekends in the pubs and restaurants downtown, even as we bought ever more organic local produce at the Flint Farmers' Market, the skeletal portents of a new decade rose around us. Doors agape, windows smashed and hollow, siding stripped, grass rising uncut before them, the houses in Flint began to look like skulls resting on a forgotten battlefield.

When the time came for us to leave, we did our best. My aunt hired a builder to come out and solidly board the place up. If we were going to abandon our home, we would leave it in as much dignity as we could. A hollow gesture, but we owed it that much. Perhaps if it was done properly, the place would be reasonably intact when the Land Bank took it over, making it a decent candidate for rehab instead of more fodder for the bulldozer. That's how I comforted myself, at least. Maybe, one day long in the future, I could come back to it.

In Flint, if you have a moving truck backed up to the door, people will just walk in. One guy wanted to rent the place. Another guy wanted to buy the HVAC gear that we had just installed the year before in a fit of reckless good intentions. We named a price. He called "his guy," who said similar gear could be had far cheaper elsewhere. Mom told him she'd rather it be stolen.

We've been gone for five years. I have not seen our house since the day I drove the U-Haul away, but I've heard through the grapevine that its siding was stripped almost on the day we left. Given the various rounds of demolitions the city has had in the intervening years, it may not even be there today. I expect I'll learn of its fate one day, but I'm in no hurry.

Abandoning a home is a curious thing. When you leave a place you have lived and loved, where hearts have grown and filled and broken, where you have trimmed Christmas trees and carved Thanksgiving turkeys and played catch into the warm nights with your friends, where you have celebrated after marriages and have sought refuge after funerals, you take solace in the fact that at least the place will go on. Others will grow to know the place as you did and may one day feel as rooted there as you do. Their ghosts will join with yours.

There will be no such future for 2302 Welch Boulevard, a modest but sturdy bungalow built to house the floodtide of the postwar American middle class. An honest structure possessed, like its neighbors, of the quiet dignity that comes with safeguarding generations through the good times and the bad.

It may seem indecent to mourn for an abandoned house, especially in a city where so many have lost so much more. But I do not think that is what I am doing when I think about our house, not precisely. I am mourning the little piece of my city that was the most mine, my refuge from the personal, social, cultural, and political turmoil that still characterizes my hometown.

Being Bama

BECKY WILSON

"Bama, the only thing you have to do in this life is stay white and die."
This was the advice of my seventh grade science teacher who, from the very first day of class, called me Bama, which was short for Alabama, which he thought was appropriate because of my voice. Apparently to him I sounded southern. To my white classmates, it meant that I sounded ghetto. Strangely enough, though, my black classmates called me Boston. They thought that I sounded eastern. Even though seventh grade ended for me in the spring of 1991, I still quiver when I hear a recording of my voice.

If walking into second hour greeted by the teacher shaking his fist chanting, "Bama, Bama" was a source of dread, then the call to stay white and die was a source of confusion. For a hormonal, depressed, junior high school girl, the dying part seemed like something to aspire to. Staying white caused my already easily distracted mind to spend hours wondering how I could stay white when I didn't even know what it meant to be white.

My lab partner was another reason to dread second-hour science. We just never hit it off. Two weeks into the school year, she had already threatened to slap me or have her mother call mine. She later apologized for being inconsiderate and mentioning a telephone as she was certain that my family was not able to afford one. She was legally blind, which in itself was not the problem. The problem was that she insisted on doing all the experiments on her own. Even though she could not see everything and often confused white wires with black wires and put washers in places that there should have been bolts, she refused to let me help. The few times I worked up the courage to talk to our teacher, his response was always the same, a fist shake followed by a "Bama, Bama, I told you what you need to do."

Being Bama was like wearing my own scarlet letter on my forehead. It matched the other one I wore, which wasn't a letter at all, but rather a number: bus route 13.

Everybody knew when I got off the bus each day that I was from *that* side of town. But until seventh grade I was unaware that there was another side of town besides mine. I was also unaware that so many others did not appreciate what they considered to be my lack of connection to my white race.

My whiteness was questioned because of my voice and also because of my hair: I began seventh grade with an unfortunate mullet. A few weeks before the start of school, I'd gone to the hair salon and asked for a "black girl cut." In my mind this meant an asymmetrical bob with a long wide tail in the back. For the old white woman cutting my hair it meant short bangs, razor short sides, and a party in the back. It only got worse months later when I let another stylist give me a spiral perm. She promised it would make me look like Mariah Carey. It only made me look like a poodle that had been left out in the rain.

My science partner didn't call me Bama or Boston, but quite often white trash. Another source of confusion. She had it wrong. The way I saw it, by living out near the county line and taking a cab to school, she fit the description more closely than me. My vision of white trash included people who lived in trailers in the woods, cheated the welfare system, stole from their families, grew pot, drank cheap liquor, and abused children. I had family members who helped shape this vision. I had other family members I never thought of as trash, but they were clearly white racists. My grandpa kept a statue of a black jockey near the front door. When we left the house he put the statue in the front window. "He'll scare them away," he'd say.

I had a friend in seventh grade whose mother didn't want her to come to my house because of the street I lived on. She had science second hour too, but in the classroom next to mine. Yes, my sister and I were the only white girls on the street, but why be angry at me for that? Be angry at the families that moved away. The street changed just as the classrooms in my elementary school had. Every year there were fewer white faces. By sixth grade there were just three of us. One of them hated me because her dad told her that "loving one is the only thing worse than being one." (Of course, this is a paraphrase. Her words were somewhat less poetic.) One day during math class, when our teacher stepped out of the room, one of our classmates put a sponge in her desk, an attempt to tell her she stunk and needed to bathe. Everyone laughed. I laughed, even though I knew how humiliated she must have felt, because I was just happy to not be the butt of the joke. While our teacher was still away from the room, the girl walked over and slapped me across the face. The sting was not as painful as the one I felt every time she called me a "n----- lover."

The following summer I had another experience that left me red in the face. This one was not in a classroom, although I could have easily spent the entire summer in school had I not pulled myself together and passed English. I had been attending church camp every summer for years. Looking back, I wonder why I ever went back after the first. Perhaps I wanted a week away from home so badly that I was willing to overlook being treated as an outcast. My fellow campers had no use for me, except of course when they needed another body on the basketball court. You wouldn't believe how many times I heard, "She's from Flint, she has to know how to play." I also heard a lot of, "She's from Flint. That's why she talks like that." I always wanted to ask (but never did) how exactly it was that I talked? I still wonder if it was the tone of my voice that evoked strong reaction or my vocabulary. Every summer that I went to camp, a friend went with me who was also from Flint. To our fellow campers from the woods, he was the only black kid they ever saw, and they all flocked to him. He was a token. I was just trash.

Sitting in the pole barn for arts and crafts time, I received a vocabulary lesson. I was at a table with several girls who really grated on my nerves, but whose approval I craved like Fun Dips and Chick-O-Sticks. I hated that they took twenty-minute showers while the line for those of us waiting grew longer and longer. I didn't take showers that long at home. I thought it was stupid that they spent so much time curling their hair and applying their eye shadow, blush, and lipstick. We're at camp, for God's sake! The girl sitting next to me making a beautiful "I love Jesus" necklace, who was also the craft coordinator's granddaughter, taught me the new word that day. And while I always enjoyed expanding my vocabulary, I was humiliated by this particular lesson. She called me a "wigger." Huh? I had never heard the word before. To be called this, for the first time, in the pole barn, at church camp, while we were making Jesus necklaces and wearing T-shirts with crosses and Bibles on the front was almost enough to make me lose my religion. Even though I knew right away what it meant, she went on to say, "You know, a wigger, someone who wants to be black."

Even though I never had that science teacher again, he continued calling me Bama when we saw each other in the hallway. We belonged to the same fitness center for a while and he shook his fist and gave me a "Bama, Bama" when we passed each other walking on the track. Seventh grade also wasn't the end of my encounters with the science partner. We had several classes together right up until graduation. We never did see eye to eye, and she never totally ceased with her "white trash" comments. She also never learned to accept my help. This was evident during home economics our senior year when she messed up our cookie dough by using the wrong size measuring cup when adding the flour to the bowl. I learned to ignore her most of the time, but I was totally grossed out when she licked the spatula and then stuck it right back in the mix. Please define "trashy."

Trash got picked up on Tuesdays on the street that was littered with remnants of racism, white flight, and poverty, the depths of which I didn't understand until I moved away. I sometimes dropped the trash bags on the curb before I walked toward the bus stop. Being bused to a school on the other side of town after attending the neighborhood school for all of my elementary years was a rough ride. The bus was overcrowded, and since my stop was one of the last, there were never any open seats by the time I got on. If we had the usual driver, she would let me sit on the top step, otherwise I had to stand. The school bus was the first time I encountered someone who wasn't white that didn't like me for being white. Up until then I thought all my black classmates thought of me as "being down." I'd never had a black classmate question my wearing a leather necklace with an engraved image of the African continent or "Dwayne Wayne sun glasses" or a pantsuit from Roglins before. In my mind I was just wearing what my friends wore, and naively didn't see why someone would take issue with my fashion style. In an attempt to be more white, I went to school one day wearing my new white K-Swiss that I'd spent all my Christmas money on, with a preppy sweater and heavy blue eye-liner, pink blush, and shiny purple lip gloss. I got up early that day, took a long shower and curled my hair. The response from the girls on the bus was not what I anticipated: "Oh, so you wanna be white now. What, you don't like us no more?" Being Bama was hard, but still easier than those nights I cried myself to sleep wondering if I'd ever know what it felt like to be me.

Today I sit in a coffee shop in Detroit and find myself staring out the window, fascinated by the waste management trucks in a parking lot across the street, emptying trash from the dumpster. On the wall there is a sign reminding customers to recycle. Who decides what is trash and what has another use?

I don't think too much anymore about my science teacher's call to "stay white." But I wonder every day what it means to "be white." There is a black woman standing on the corner in front of the coffee shop begging for change. I haven't seen anyone put a dime in her hand. There is a black man sitting on the curb hunched over, not wearing any shoes, who the police just told to move along. There is a group of black teenagers waiting for the bus. One of the young women is wearing a shirt with an image of the African continent imprinted on it. A white woman crossed the street seemingly to avoid them. At least today, "being white" means being welcome in this coffee shop without suspicion and being able to walk down the street without being followed by the police or feared by pedestrians. It means I can afford to spend $5 on a lavender latte. I hear a young white woman at another table say that it was a real adjustment moving into the city and how it was more difficult than she imagined, living and working with people of other races.

I visited Alabama earlier this year to see a friend. I didn't hear anyone with a voice like mine. If I'm not asking what it means to be and to sound like Bama, maybe I'm free to finally find out what it means to be and to sound like me.

Too Fancy for Flint?

ANDREW MORTON

I live in Flint. I own a home in the city. However, I'm still often reluctant to call Flint my home. This isn't because I'm not madly in love with this place, or incredibly proud to live in the city. It's because of the way I talk.

As soon as I open my mouth, most people realize I'm clearly not from here. What comes out of my mouth is a sort of transatlantic mess—the result of spending approximately half of my life in the U.K., where I was born, and the rest in the middle of Michigan, America's high five.

Whenever I meet new people, either in Flint or elsewhere, as soon as people realize that I'm British and that I live in Flint, their first response is usually, "Why?" I'm always puzzled by and slightly amused at the reactions I get. For the most part they always seem to suggest that Flint, Michigan, is clearly not good enough, or fancy enough, for a British person. Obviously this is based on a lot of tired stereotypes of the British, which I blame mostly on PBS.

So how did I end up in Flint? The short version of the story goes like this: my father is an engineer, his company transferred him to Michigan in the mid-nineties, we eventually settled in a suburb of Flint, and in an attempt to assimilate—and because my older brother was one—the thirteen-year-old me decided to become a skateboarder. We soon learned that there are a lot of cool places to skate in and around downtown Flint, and the rest is history.

That's also the cooler version of the story. What I left out of the first version is that I was raised in the Salvation Army, and when my family moved to the States we began attending the Salvation Army Flint Citadel Church on Kearsley Street in downtown Flint. This was really my first introduction to the city. At that time, there really wasn't much happening downtown. The general consensus was that it was a dangerous place, and one that you should avoid at all costs. Most people at the Church would simply drive in for Sunday services and weeknight activities, and then return home to the suburbs or the "nicer" parts of Flint afterwards. However, as I gradually began to spend more time exploring the city, I never felt scared when I was downtown. Perhaps it was my youthful naieveté. The more likely reason was the fact that I rarely saw any other people—and when I did encounter people downtown, they were usually friendly.

It was at some point during this period that Flint first began to get under my skin. After graduating high school I studied theater at the University of Michigan-Flint, located in the heart of downtown. I lived at home for the first couple of years, but then moved into an apartment with some friends in the East Village, a small neighborhood nestled between the UM-Flint campus and the Flint Cultural Center. During the four years I was a student I taught after-school reading programs at both Cook and King Elementary Schools, both of which—like many of Flint's schools— are now closed. For a while I delivered sandwiches and got to know people who worked in the various offices downtown. One summer I helped run a summer youth employment program through the Michigan Community Service Corps, and during another I helped plant a garden on the corner of Martin Luther King Boulevard and 5th Avenue—the unofficial border between downtown and North Flint.

During these four years, I slowly came to see a different side of the United States. Growing up in England, my only insight into American culture was what I saw on TV. Just as many of my American friends based their understanding of British culture from what they watched on PBS, I grew up watching shows like *Saved by the Bell* and *The Fresh Prince of Bel-Air*. When we moved to the U.S., my family lived in hotel for almost a month before we found a place to live. My brother and I spent most of those days watching a ridiculous amount of cable television, exploring the mall across the road, and eating out most evenings. We thought it was great. It felt like we were living the life of the characters from our favorite shows. However, once I began to experience Flint in new ways, I began to see the other America. The one we never saw on TV growing up in England.

I started college thinking I wanted to be an actor. Four years later I knew that was no longer the case, but I wasn't certain what I wanted to do instead. But I began to recognize a pattern in a lot of my part-time and summer jobs. All attempted to address some of the larger social and economic issues facing communities like Flint: illiteracy, poverty, blight. For a while I thought perhaps I would become a teacher or a social worker, but I couldn't quite give up the idea of wanting to do something in theater. Towards the end of my time at UM-Flint, Judy Rosenthal, an anthropology professor, suggested I read Augusto Boal's *Theatre of the Oppressed*. I did, and found what I had been looking for. The thought of creating theater that could highlight the injustices in the world and demand change energized me, and I was hungry for more.

In 2004, I graduated from the University of Michigan-Flint. It was looking fairly certain that George W. Bush was going to be re-elected, and despite my family being well and truly settled in Michigan, I wasn't too happy with the direction the country was going in. I remember many nights at the Torch Bar & Grill in Buckham Alley—a dive bar still frequented by the members of Flint's small, but faithful theatre scene—when friends joked about how they wanted to move to Canada, or England, or anywhere where a Bush wasn't in power. As I still had my British passport and family back in the U.K., I had an exit strategy, so I took it.

I had also been accepted into a relatively new masters program at Goldsmiths College, part of the University of London. It was a program in Community Arts, designed for artists who wanted to create work in and with diverse communities, and often outside of the traditional arts sector. So in the summer of 2004, I went back across the pond, and found a new home in South London.

To the surprise of a lot of Americans I met when I first moved to the States, I didn't grow up in London. I was born in Derby, a midsize city in the Midlands (roughly two hours north of London). When I moved to the big smoke, I knew no one. I found a room to rent in a Victorian Terrace house on a street that overlooked a park that was only a short walk away from the Goldsmiths campus. As I was studying part-time, I took a job folding over-priced T-shirts in an Urban Outfitters on Oxford Street—the busiest shopping street in London. However, it wasn't very long before that job began to eat away at my soul. I started looking for new work, and to my luck the school across the street from my house, Deptford Park Primary School, was looking for teaching assistants. I got the job, said goodbye to folding T-shirts, and soon realized that while a part of me had run away from Flint, I had inadvertently found Flint in London.

Deptford Park was a school located in the middle of a large social housing estate—the Pepys Estate, named after the noted 17th-century diarist Samuel Pepys. During the time I worked at the school, the estate was the subject of a BBC documentary called *The Tower: A Tale of Two Cities*. In an attempt to fund regeneration of other parts of the estate, the local council had sold one of the towers (the one with the best views of the Thames) to a private developer. As that tower was redeveloped into luxury apartments, the residents of the rest of the estate struggled with crime, heroin abuse, and many other issues that often plague residents of low-income communities.

I quickly fell in love with this little community and many of the people I met there. The students I worked with reminded me very much of many of the young people I worked with in Flint. They were bright, energetic and eager to learn. The teachers and other support staff at the school knew that the estate (and the school) had a bad reputation, but they fought hard against this, and worked tirelessly to make the school a safe and supportive environment for everyone there. They too reminded me of many of my friends who I had left behind in Flint.

It was also during these few years in London that I first begin to seriously explore playwriting. I signed up for a young writers course at the Royal Court Theatre, a London theatre that had been championing new work and new voices since it was founded in the fifties, and during a ten week writing course I begin writing what I consider to be my first "real" play. It was called *February*. It was set in Flint, and inspired in part by the fatal shooting of six-year old Kayla Rolland in Beecher (just north of Flint) in 2000, and my own experiences working briefly in various Flint schools.

I still remember the day I got the phone call from the theater telling me that the play had been shortlisted for their young writers festival. I answered the call on my cellphone on a busy street near Goldsmiths, and ducked into a phone booth so I could hear better. They told me they were interested in developing my play. I said thank you, hung up, and burst into happy tears. A theater I admired was interested in my play about Flint, Michigan! I immediately began rewriting, trying desperately to make it what I thought the Royal Court wanted. But the results were dismal. Like many works of art made about Flint, the play portrayed the city as a bleak, hopeless place from which people are desperate to escape. Many people I met in London already had this image of Flint in their minds, thanks mostly to Michael Moore's *Roger & Me*, and my work didn't challenge this perception, it simply reinforced it.

Eventually the theater passed on the play. They called with the bad news on what was meant to be my last official day of work at Deptford Park. I stepped out of a classroom to take the call, and then went and sobbed in the art supply closet.

Shortly after completing my masters program, I begin running the young people's theatre project at the Blue Elephant Theatre in Camberwell, another South London community that like Deptford, reminded me very much of Flint. I stayed for three years, and gradually took on more projects, including creating a theater program with residents of the Bethwin Estate, and running the Speak Out Forum Theatre Project, making work that explored many of the systemic problems facing young people in London.

For a while, it felt like I was making a new life for myself in London. I was creating theatre that I felt made a difference, and I was beginning to wonder if I would stay there for good. But Flint was very much on my mind. I still had a Green Card, granting me permission to live and work in the U.S., and on a trip back to the States for my brother's wedding, an immigration officer began to ask questions about where I was living. I was informed that if I wanted to keep the Green Card, I would need to return permanently to the U.S., or I'd be asked to surrender it.

After months of agonizing, making multiple pros/cons lists, and seeking guidance from close friends over multiple evenings at the pub, I finally bit the bullet and decided to return to the States. While I was happy with the life I was making for myself in London, I realized that I didn't feel ready to commit to living in the U.K. forever. While I was living in London, a former professor of mine from UM-Flint, Dr. Lauren Friesen, brought several groups of theater students to London for a month for a study abroad trip. I would meet with them, to talk about my work, and during one visit I mentioned the possibility that I might be back in the States in the future. Friesen said that if I ever ended up back in Flint he'd love to have me teach some classes at UM-Flint. I returned to Michigan in the spring of 2010, and began teaching my first classes in the summer semester.

I didn't think I would be in Flint for very long. I thought I'd teach for a year or so and explore my options. When in London, I loved being in a large cosmopolitan city. I assumed I'd maybe make the move to New York or Chicago, but it's now almost six years since I came back to Flint, and I'm still here. I still teach part-time at UM-Flint, and for the past three years I've also been working at the Flint Youth Theatre, where I am now the playwright in residence. I don't know if I'll be here forever, but for the time being, it does feel like this is where I need to be.

I don't say this to suggest Flint needs people like me (a gay, white British guy who makes theatre). The story of how I ended up here still confuses plenty of people, but it makes a lot of sense to me. I know now I couldn't have done the work I did in Deptford and Camberwell without the experiences I had growing up in Flint, and I know I couldn't do what I do in Flint today without the lessons I learned in the six years I was away. Flint could quite easily do without me, but I don't know how I would fare if Flint wasn't still a huge part of my life.

I'm still writing plays, many of which are very much about Flint. I've written about the impact of arson on the city, the anti-democratic Emergency Manager legislation passed by Governor Rick Snyder and the response by activists in the city, and the rise in vacant city lots being transformed into community gardens. While I consider *February* the Flint play I needed to write in order to learn what kind of play I didn't want to write, I had to return to the city before I could finally find the plays that had been escaping me for so long.

I'm going to turn thirty-four later this year. Very soon I'll have spent more of my life in the Flint area than I have in the U.K. Despite not having the honor of being born in this place, I do feel like the city is my adopted home. I'm very protective of Flint; I'll defend it whenever necessary, and I now see how instrumental this city has been in making me the person and artist I am today. However, I still feel slightly uncomfortable claiming that I'm from here, and I think this is because I feel like I haven't done enough to earn that distinction.

The fact that I choose to remain in Flint sets me apart from the significant number of residents who would like to leave but, for many complex reasons, are unable to. I also understand why not everyone feels the same way about this place as I do. I'm fascinated by those with questionable ties to this place who still embrace the "Flint identity," perhaps because they think it makes them appear tough, or cool. However if you're going to claim this identity, you need to earn it. You need to understand and be willing to grapple with the complexities of this community, and be willing to put in the effort to help make this place more just and equitable for everyone who lives here. Being able to claim Flint is a badge of honor, and one that I'm still in the process of earning.

Flint is more than good enough, and certainly fancy enough for a British guy like me. The question I still constantly ask myself, though, is this: Am I good enough for Flint?

ANDREW MORTON

Do You Realize?

LAYLA MEILLIER

Sometimes, I wish I could turn off my awareness and explore without the worry of fight or flight. I have permanent eyes in the back of my head from growing up in Flint. Granted, I feel safer because of my hyperawareness, but some days I wish I could just let myself meander.

I started practicing my meander when I would walk home from school, and trust that the daylight and the camaraderie of the city would keep me safe—a sort of personal experiment. I would turn my music all the way up and force myself to look at the flowers, trash, and concrete veins in the sidewalk.

One day in particular, while I was listening to the Flaming Lips' "Do You Realize?" I looked up and there was a man a block away. I'm not one to judge, but I knew this man was the reason meandering went out of style in Flint. He faced me in head-on confrontation, spread his legs, straddled the sidewalk. *How odd*, I thought. But I forced myself to trust him. I kept walking forward at the same pace. I even looked off to the side casually like there was something interesting going on across the street. When I looked back, his eyes remained on me.

I was half a block away when he pulled out a gun and pointed it straight at me, cocked his head. *Here we go*, I thought. I had really done it this time. I had nowhere to duck to. I approached an infamous patch of broken glass on the sidewalk, considered picking up the pieces for defense, but something made me walk right over it and miss my opportunity. I kept walking straight towards him. I was carrying a milk-white calculus book; I imagined it stained with my blood. Would my mother have to pay for the cost of this book if I died, or would they take pity on her and hold the bill? Ten feet now, I spread my arms wide. We lock eyes.

Six feet, I discover his gun is real.

Five feet, I have no goodbyes to say.

Three feet, here I go, dying in the middle of the day.

Two feet, silence in my head.

I meet the barrel. It was pointing at the meeting of my collarbones the entire time. "Are you scared?" he says. I mug him as best I can in my numb state.

"No." My voice is strangely firm.

He steps out of my way, puts away his gun.

"Are you a student?" He motions toward my books.

"Yes." My voice is no longer firm.

"What are you studying?"

"English."

He gives me a "huh," a smile, and then runs to catch the bus. I watch him as he bouncily climbs the steps and then turns around to shout from the doorway, "Wait, how old are you?"

"Twenty," I yell back to him and watch as his bus leaves.

I was sixteen at the time.

Do you realize that you have the most beautiful face?
Do you realize we're floating in space?
Do you realize that happiness makes you cry?
Do you realize that everyone you know someday will die?
And instead of saying all of your goodbyes, let them know
You realize that life goes fast
It's hard to make the good things last
You realize the sun doesn't go down
It's just an illusion caused by the world spinning round...

That was a little over two years ago and I am still not sure how many times I can get so lucky.

The previous winter I was walking home from school on the same route during the same time of day, and I watched a man get shot. I had heard plenty of shots, felt them shake my house, but never before watched a man, in the open, get hit with a spark and go down.

I was passing a brick church when I noticed two men in the parking lot, heave-hoing a long, awkward, black bag into a commercial sized garbage bin. I stopped, backed up, and hid behind the brick. I watched with an eighth of my body not protected by the wall. I knew the "trash'" was one large object. My imagination told me it was a body. When they set fire to the bin, my imagination sung, "I told ya so." The fire spread high quickly and before anyone knew it, the fire engines were whistling around the corner. The two men looked at each other in an attempt to formulate a wordless plan. The engines sped closer, the one furthest from me panicked. He shot the other man. I took flight. I have never run so fast in my entire life. I passed the men, the flaming bin. I did not even pause to see if the crosswalk was safe, I almost got hit by the snout of the fire truck. I ran all the way home and did not stop until I was up the stairs and to the window to see if anyone had followed me. Tears froze on my face, my mouth tasted like snot and fear. My nerves did not settle for days.

So, I wish—so very badly—that I could just not see the man crossing the street three blocks away, I wish I could avoid eye contact with the man sitting on the curb, I want so badly to not speed ahead and check nooks and crannies when I am out walking with a group of friends. But the older I get, the more I accomplish with my life, the more I build my savings account, and write painfully personal things in my journal, the more I realize I cannot let my guard falter for shits and giggles. Life is too delicate, time is too important, and starting over is just too much work.

I have a friend from Flint, a lifetime resident. She gets it. She says, "I feel safer because I live in Flint." Living in this city prepares you for things you didn't even know you had to prepare for. Maybe it comes down to paying for your kid's swimming lessons or dropping them in the pool; maybe it's a question of how close you can get to the "wrong end" of the human condition before it ultimately kills you.

I'm not entirely sure. Until I figure it out, I might as well meander.

When Home Says, "Go"

SARAH CARSON

I n 1997, an international incident was brewing.

The World Wrestling Federation's Shawn Michaels and Hunter Hearst Helmsley had declared war on their Canadian rivals, the Hart Foundation.

Their new faction, Degeneration X, was set to battle the Harts just forty-five minutes west of where I—all of thirteen years old—was living with my mother and sister in a suburb of Flint, Michigan.

My mom, a sensible woman who did not waste her Monday nights watching grown men pretend to fight on the USA Network, offered me a deal.

She'd be happy to pay for me to watch this ridiculous display—in fact she'd be happy to pay for me and a friend and a friend's parent to watch it—if only the friend's parent would do the driving and chaperoning.

My mother would, under no circumstances whatsoever, sit through a professional wrestling event.

"Deal!" I thought. "No problem! Perfect!"

I got on the phone to my best friend and relayed the offer: an all-expenses paid trip to the defining moment of our young wrestling fandom. Sexy boy himself Shawn Michaels! Sweet chin music! Triple H and the Pedigree! Those despicable Canadians coming through the curtains, off the ropes, a folding chair to the back of their heads! We could see it all! All we needed was a ride.

I heard my friend put down the phone and call to her mother in another room beyond the phone cord's reach.

"I don't know how to get to Lansing," her mother said. "I've never been farther west than Durand."

There was quiet as my lungs, my friend's lungs, deflated.

My friend pleaded. She conveyed our desperation.

But her mother was stalwart: "No way," she said. "I am not leaving Flint."

It's been nearly two decades since I did not see Shawn Michaels and Triple H defeat the Hart Foundation, and nearly a decade since I packed my things and left my hometown, left my family and friends and elementary school and baptismal church and favorite playground and roller-skating rink and front-porch-of-my-first-kiss.

And it's taken just about that long for me to understand why my friend's mom refused to take us to Lansing that day.

I've lived in Chicago for nearly ten years, and if the people I meet now have heard of Flint, they've heard of violence, they've heard of lead-poisoned water.

Of course they've heard about the birth of General Motors, the Great Sit-Down Strike, but mostly they've heard about plants closing, homes set on fire, generations of families out of work.

But what they've not heard is that no one leaves home unless leaving home is a necessity, unless home is a set fire burning too hot to go back.

What I most struggle to explain to the people I know now is what I think people from the Bronx, from Chicago's South Side, from Texas, from Mexico must also struggle to explain—that there's a kind of pride in being from somewhere other people do not want to be from, that there are entire families, blocks, neighborhoods who've never thought about leaving, whose identity is rooted in the fact that they've stayed.

My family is one of those families, whose tree is almost entirely rooted in thirty square miles, who was Vehicle City before Vehicle City was a thing.

My great-grandfather built Buicks. My father's father built Buicks. My father built Buicks when he was not arguing with the foreman about his Ted Nugent poster.

My grandmother built Buicks. My mother's father won a lapel pin by building Buicks, by having the cleanest station in the spring shop.

When my mom first showed me *Roger and Me*, I never dreamed of becoming an expatriate, an out-of-state resident, an absentee voter, a girl in search of a hometown.

Except that home became a place unrecognizable from the photos my mother keeps in neatly-stacked boxes. Except that home welcomed me into its warm, wet mouth just to spit me as far as its tongue could launch me. Except home looked me in the eyes and asked me to leave.

It starts with a dog.

Maybe it starts a little before the dog. Maybe it starts in college, where I first learned that it could be done, that survival away from home was possible, even if it meant getting used to people who didn't know the difference between a Detroit and a Flint coney, who have no moral qualms about financing a Toyota, who have never missed a phone bill in their lives.

But mostly it starts on my grandma's living room floor, just north of the Pierson Road Meijer that has since been torn down to the pavement, just west of the Ramada Inn that has also been leveled, not far from a Denny's that is no longer there.

It starts twenty-two years after I was born at Flint Osteopathic Hospital, twenty-four years after my mother was also born at Flint Osteopathic Hospital, sixty-one years after my grandmother was born at home where Lavelle and Flushing Roads meet.

It starts just after I had come back to Flint from my first failed attempt at adulthood in Southeast Michigan, after my mom had paid the adoption fees for a sad-looking hound dog picked up by Genesee County Animal Control, after I flipped through a Bible trying to find a name worthy of a dog whose story was as epic as the story of the patriarchs.

The dog had been found abandoned in a house on the east side, in what I liked to imagine was a warm, Sears Roebuck bungalow, one of the thousands of houses erected quickly for factory families, families who'd come north on the promise of work on the assembly lines, not far from where my dad had spent thirty years behind the controls of a crane, hoisting dyes for Regals and Sport Wagons, near where Grandma had moved into her first apartment with Grandpa after leaving her first husband alone on the farm.

The dog needed a name that said all this each time he was called. He needed a name that would always bring him back to where he came from.

Abraham? The father of many nations?

David? The giant slayer? The boy who'd become king?

No, this dog wasn't a ruler as much as a harbinger, a marker of a moment, carrying with him a warning about how the past becomes us, takes us over.

I named him Amos, after God's man in the fields, the watcher of fig trees with an admonition for all those who'd listen—a warning about exile, about repeating the past, about a way of life that was not coming back.

Amos and I only looked at two houses before signing our very own lease on Flint, Michigan.

The first was in Little Missouri, just east of the expressway, owned by a little elderly couple that lived next door and seemed too interested in how much time I might be around to help them change light bulbs.

The second, on Lexington Avenue, half a block from the Grand Trunk bridge, across from a dime store, lumber yard and muffler shop that are all vacant real estate now, came with a rent-to-own contract and the promise of a chain-link fence for the dog.

The tiny one-bedroom had high vaulted ceilings where the owner, Darwin—another never-left-Flint kind of guy who'd worked as a detective before opening his own private investigation business—had drywalled over the attic. Grapevines crawled up a back fence that separated our lawn from a junkyard. Oak trees grew the perfect distance from each other to hang a hammock. Two steel poles marked where a clothesline once stood.

Darwin told me he'd paint the house whatever colors I liked. He wrote our lease on a loose piece of floral stationary.

"What's a good-looking girl like you doing moving into a house alone, anyway?" he asked as he handed me the keys.

"I'm not alone," I smiled. "I have Amos."

Amos followed his nose around the backyard and began digging a path under the fence.

In Flint in 2006, the year Amos and I moved into our one-bedroom house, the city-data.com crime rate was 1089.6. That means that—figuratively—for every 100,000 people living in Flint, 1,089 of them would have been affected by a serious or violent crime. This is more than three times the U.S. average of 294.

In 2006, fifty-four people were murdered in Flint. 2,246 were assaulted. 3,058 houses were burgled.

On nights when Amos and I would go eat TV dinners with my grandmother, after she'd cleared the plates, after she'd lit up a menthol Smoker's Choice, after Amos had his own snack of Cheerios and peanut butter, Grandma would grab the remote and announce, "Let's see who got killed today" as she turned on the evening news.

So perhaps I should not have been surprised the first time I heard the rumor about masked men creeping through the neighborhood.

I'd only been in my house a month when so-and-so told so-and-so who told so-and-so who told me about the retired bus driver with the grown children in Florida who sometimes did her cooking naked with the back door open—how she hadn't heard the knocking at her door, so the masked men had let themselves in through a window. They made off with her jewelry and her television and promised not to hurt her if she didn't call the cops.

Soon after the same story was being told about Mercedes in the house across the street, whose toddler son spent all day running naked back and forth across the yard—sometimes through the sprinkler, sometimes for no reason at all. She had opened the door for the men and let them take what they wanted.

Whether they actually had pistols or were only pretending by holding their fingers taut inside their jacket pockets was unclear.

But each morning they were at a new house, coming to the back doors rather than the front.

"It's your dog that's kept them away from you," the neighbors told me. "They know you've got a dog and don't want to mess with him."

It was a comforting idea, but I didn't buy it.

On the north side, both my aunt and uncle's dogs had been shot in their front yard when masked men had come calling. The only difference, I figured, was that the masked men who'd turned up at my aunt and uncle's had an agenda.

I was sure our masked men were also people who had never left Flint. Being anything else required a plan.

This, of course, had all happened in summer, when everyone knows things are crazy, when everyone expects a little drama, a little violence, a little heat-induced stupid followed by a lot of summertime dumb.

When fall came, the city mellowed. The firecracker pop of gunshots to the north lessened. I met a boy who'd just gotten out of the Thumb Correctional Facility on a gun trafficking charge, and he offered me all his love in addition to all his weed.

I took a job selling Faygo to party stores up and down Saginaw Street and Linden and Corunna Roads. I spent my breaks at work writing poems in the cab of the van, dispatches from grocery store backrooms and tractor-trailers full of soda.

Amos and I worked to fix up our little bungalow. I retiled the kitchen floor. I wallpapered the bathroom. Amos learned not to pee on the rug.

Then in January some guys threw a chunk of concrete through the Faygo van window and stole my cell phone and purse while I was in a store taking an order.

The Sikh brothers who owned the place let me watch the whole incident on their closed-circuit recording system.

"Such a shame," they said, shaking their turbaned heads.

One night in February, while Amos and I sat curled on the couch watching Judge Judy tell two feuding roommates what was what, I heard footsteps on my front porch and peeked through the blinds to see a stranger in a fedora trying to get an eyeline into my window.

Bolstered by Judge Judy's no-nonsense spirit, I called, "What do you want?" through the blinds.

"Is Mercedes here?" he yelled back.

Before I could answer, a police SUV appeared at the curb. Two officers made their way up my sidewalk. They slammed the stranger against the glass of my storm door and ordered him to spread his legs.

"Do you know this guy?" a cop called to me through the closed window.

"No," I replied.

"Make sure your door is locked," the cop instructed.

I don't know what happened after that. It didn't seem in my best interest to watch.

One Christmas, years after I had moved away from Flint, I asked Grandma to tell me the story of how she met Grandpa.

She told me her mother had wanted her to marry a guy named Howard, whose family had a large farm, who could provide a good life for Grandma.

And Grandma did marry Howard, but Howard was annoying. So Grandma left him and started working at Buick during World War II, when the factory was co-opted to make airplane parts rather than cars. Grandpa worked on the line with her. They started flirting. Then dating. Then they moved in together even though Grandma was still technically married to Howard. She divorced Howard and married Grandpa, and they bought a house together in Beecher, a neighborhood on the north end of Flint, a neighborhood Michael Moore made famous in *Bowling for Columbine* with the story of Kayla Rolland, the youngest school shooting victim in United States history.

Grandma told me about the house, how at times they had crammed more than ten people into its two tiny bedrooms, how the church had given them piles of free dishes that didn't match.

She told me about the 1953 tornado that leveled that house. How Grandpa, unable to get past the downed trees on Belsay Road, had abandoned the car and run home on foot to find Aunt Anna thrown clear across the yard onto the roof of the chicken coop.

She told me how the whole family had slept in a tent in the yard until they could afford to get the house fixed.

She paused.

Then she said, "You know, this town just isn't the same town as it used to be."

By spring of my first year back in Flint, I'd made a habit of only putting a couple of dollars of gas into my car at a time and constantly running the gas tank dry.

One night I was on my way to a downtown pop-up art show when I couldn't get the car to start. I grabbed a gas can and started walking down Fenton Road toward the Stop and Shop.

It was pitch black. The streetlights that worked burned faint orange. I passed a boarded up muffler shop, a boarded up used bookstore.

Despite the many reasons I had to be, though, I still don't remember being afraid.

The masked men, the police on the porch, the stolen cell phone—none of it had been particularly frightening.

Even the night I called the cops because I could hear someone breaking out car windows down the street, and the 911 dispatcher laughed at me for calling, I wasn't particularly scared. I was just tired. Just tired and wide awake.

Then that night, as I rounded the corner of the library annex, I heard the sound of grown men yelling. Then came the pop-pop-pop of gunfire. Then the sound of tires squealing, of someone getting away.

I curled myself in the library doorway for what seemed like forever, sure that they'd return, that they'd need to dispose of the witnesses.

That night at home, I scratched Amos' belly in the darkness, and I thought of my friend's mom who refused to take us to see Shawn Michaels.

But even then I hadn't understood why she hadn't wanted to take us downstate, why she'd never left Flint, why so many of us had never tried to live anywhere else.

Only years later did I realize that the violence, the strangers on the porch, the police who didn't come when called, the gunshots—they were scary, and they were dangerous—but they were no more scary or dangerous than what could be out beyond the city limits.

At least here we knew what we'd gotten ourselves into. The streets, the neighborhoods, all the unspoken agreements we made when we walked down the sidewalk were familiar.

Maybe there were other places out there where you didn't have to take cover in a library doorway just to fill a gas can.

But at least I knew the library doorway.

How would I ever find the right doorway to duck into someplace else?

In Flint, the limits were clear. The boundaries established.

Maybe it was not the same city I'd been born into, the city I'd been promised. But it was a city I knew how to navigate, even if navigating meant running for my life.

I only eventually began thinking about leaving the night I met the masked men myself.

It was spring, and it was dark outside. I hooked Amos to his leash for a walk, stepped out onto the sidewalk, and there they were, carrying a television across my neighbor's lawn.

I locked eyes with one of them. We both paused. Then I turned around and walked back inside.

I turned out all the lights. I did not call the cops. But I decided I liked my things too much to let other people break in and sell them for whatever they were selling other people's things for.

Darwin was pissed when I told him Amos and I had found an apartment in Chicago.

"I wouldn't have put up a fence," he said. "I wouldn't have painted, installed the carpet."

"I'm bored," I told him, too proud to admit defeat.

"What about the rec center?" he said. "Do you know how to play pool? I'm sure you could meet some people your age. A nice guy."

But it was over. It had been twelve months.

Again and again, the city seemed to be saying: "Go."

In Chicago, Amos and I moved into a neighborhood we thought would be a lot like Flint—working class, populated with families and young people looking for an inexpensive place to stay, in need of a new coat of paint.

But Chicago was nothing like where we'd come from. It was split by ethnicity, by socioeconomics, by baseball teams. There was no swapping of shop stories, no common connection born out of hard work—first in the factory, then in the streets—no arguing about who was from Chicago and who wasn't.

Chicago pride was different. Anyone could have it—not like in Flint where pride was hard earned.

One night I went to at an open mic at a coffee shop just north of the city and read a poem about that man in the fedora who showed up on my porch looking for Mercedes.

When I was through, I was approached by a sweet old lady, a graduate of Harvard, a resident of the uber-rich North Shore, the founder of one of Chicago's longest-lived literary magazines.

"It's a different life, isn't it?" she said to me.

I smiled. And I was overcome with loneliness. I wanted to be home more than I'd ever wanted to be home before.

It was a different life, indeed. We were only four hours down the road from Flint, but we were so far from home it was scary—far scarier than a couple of guys carrying a TV in the night.

But we learned. We adjusted.

And I started telling my story to anyone who'd listen.

I talked about fires. I talked about factories. I talked about family.

I promised I never would have left except that home had become unrecognizable, a question mark.

I started playing with a theory about what it meant to leave, about all those others like me who I'd meet in Chicago, in Kansas City, in California.

I started wondering if there weren't only three kinds of people from Flint: those who've always been there, those who've come back, and those who've gone.

I started wondering if Amos and I weren't meant to be all three.

Garden Party

NIC CUSTER

T he smell of succulent pork lured neighbors off their porches to drop by and fill a plate. Cars lined both sides of Illinois Avenue and a twenty-eight-foot-long party bus was proudly parked at the center of it all. An unmistakable graffiti mural spanned the driver's side, depicting the Flint skyline and a giant peace sign sandwiched between wild style lettering spelling out "the" and "mob."

Like most days, a fire pit glowed orange, casting late afternoon shadows off the log seating surrounding it. Our free range chicken strutted down the street past the busy crack house next door to Phil's Pepto-Bismol pink Colonial and its sagging porch where we sat two years earlier and dreamed of building an oasis.

Friends, family, and neighbors ate together, celebrating Peace Mob Gardens' bright future. It was August and the last day of our official 2011 gardening season, harvest day. Pounds of vegetables sat piled on a weathered picnic table and more hung ripe among rows of six-foot-tall sunflowers and cornstalks. Plump purple heirloom tomatoes and herb gardens, in full bloom, gave the vacant lot a jungle appeal. The 40' by 100' garden plot was a showcase of edible and ornamental plants. Dill, onions, berries, and flowers faced the sidewalk next to scraggly heads of lettuce grown in the shape of a peace sign. Hops vines climbed twenty feet of twine strung from old TV antenna towers Quikcreted into the ground. Kids chased each other down winding paths of reclaimed bricks hauled from neighborhood arsons, and two surviving pigs, picked up off Craigslist, stood peacefully penned behind donated wood fencing on Phil's front lawn. They quietly rooted in the mud, seemingly content to be rid of a bigger, aggressive male pig, which had spent the last summer bullying them and had spent the last day cooking on a spit. Vibrant yellow signs nailed to parkway trees cautioned cars to slow down for neighborhood children; one tree was adorned with dozens of donated birdhouses like an outdoor chandelier.

After two seasons, our group of twenty- and thirty-somethings had accumulated three vacant lots. On one of them, we stored our tools in a battered garage we painted barn door red. Who did what over the years kind of blurs together; each one of us contributed something unique and necessary toward moving the entire project forward. We built a water catchment system behind the garage (which we called our barn) using gutters, pickle barrels, and cinder blocks. Next door, a row of vertical pallets passively processed compost into nutrient-rich soil for the garden. As the project gained momentum and local notoriety, more talented individuals joined to create a small village worth of activity. Everybody had a role they could serve; some folks were natural born marketers and got tens of volunteers to help with a simple phone call or text. Others were political and social activists who worked to develop cooperative organizations and experimented with self-sustainability. Many of the workers were also artists who would contribute by beautifying the block. In addition to colorful educational signs, they painted houses and prepped for demolition by installing acrylic trees, poetry, and peace signs to deter lighter-happy arsonists from inadvertently contaminating the garden. We were loud, we were messy, and we wanted to create something unexpected to bring smiles to our neighbors' faces.

After a few summers of false starts near downtown, we were looking for a way to lead by example and hopefully make a big change in the community. One day in March 2010, a friend suggested we start near his house on the eastside.

Phil lived on the 1400 block of Illinois Avenue across the street from an arson that had become an overgrown dumping zone. His vision was to start a community garden that could bring a little pride back to the block. He had already invited a master gardener and her daughter to move into a small house he owned on the corner. We began cleaning up the lot's debris during the day and when it got dark, we hung out on Phil's porch, drinking beer and dreaming about the future. Two dumpsters and a few weeks later, we had torn down chain link fences and hauled in forty-two truck beds full of manure from a horse farm to begin building up good soil. The better part of a month was spent layering compost and newspapers on the polluted lot. We focused on a few adjoining lots and began to see the neighborhood as a place where we could do a lot of good with some sweat equity and very little money. Our vision evolved to creating a low-cost model for stabilizing abandoned properties, which could be replicated in other neighborhoods.

By the time we started planting that first year, we already had a plan for moving things forward and identified Genesee County Land Bank-owned properties sitting empty near the garden that we wanted to occupy. We inquired about adopting and purchasing the properties to grow the garden project. Our group was ready to make a commitment and the surrounding homes were within a few hundred dollars of being made livable. But Land Bank officials were reluctant to sell, and asked that we lease and maintain the lots for several years first to show our commitment. By the middle of that first summer, we had staked interest on land stretching across five city blocks. We felt like rock stars and kept pushing the limits of what we could do with limited donations.

Over the summers we were a featured site on two annual Edible Flint bus tours around the city. We hosted Ann Arbor grad students, Youthquest, and scout troops, showing them what was possible with a little vision and hard work. We became de facto babysitters for neighborhood kids whose parents would kick them out of the house during the day. We taught them to plant seeds, paint signs, and do small things to feel useful. Slowly though, the kids all moved away and were replaced by more empty homes.

The garden lot was at the center of the project and surrounded by a horse-shoe-shaped blot of five abandoned houses. As we started trying to secure all the adjacent empty homes, we struggled to watch over them as other neighbors swept through and scrapped their interiors, ripping out metal plumbing, water heaters, and a cast iron, claw foot bathtub. All but one of the houses was wrecked beyond reasonable repair. That last house happened to face Indiana Avenue closest to our only direct neighbor, a retiree who we will call Harry. He had spent much of his adult life in the neighborhood, surrounded by these declining houses.

He and his wife had nearly given up on the hardscrabble neighborhood, but having a group of energetic young people cleaning up the block encouraged them to stay. Initially the relationship with Harry was friendly. During the first year of our project, he helped pull out tree stumps, ripping off his beat up truck's bumper in the process. But as time wore on, Harry became increasingly irritated with our constant presence and loud celebrations.

One hungover morning I awoke in the pink house to the sound of heavy equipment rolling over the sidewalk across the street, ready to rip through the abandoned houses. Dust shot into the sky as the walls were pulled down; the wood-framed siding cracked like a bundle of sticks through a megaphone. A city employee in a hard hat hosed down the wreck as it ejected moldy plaster dust and asbestos into the garden. This was a long-desired result of federal Neighborhood Stabilization Funds (NSP2) funding dozens of Flint demolitions, including five houses facing our slice of Illinois Avenue and two facing Indiana Avenue. We offered Harry first dibs on the properties on either side of his home if he would allow us to take the three facing Illinois Avenue. He agreed, purchased the newly vacant lot next to his house and decided he wanted to build a new garage on the site. But after getting a pricey estimate, he changed his mind.

During the intervening winter, the three contiguous lots facing Illinois were our group's biggest opportunity to make a change and put Flint back on a few maps. Group members spent the winter planning to use two of the lots to build a hobbit house-style earthship as a demonstration project to kick off our larger sustainable housing cooperative. Excited, they even built a wooden scale model of the structure. Everything seemed set for success by early spring, until Harry casually bragged that he had purchased our land from under us. As it turns out, while we had been cleaning and maintaining the properties as a sign of good faith before the Land Bank would let us purchase them, Harry was dreaming up other plans.

He had sent in purchase applications for the properties surrounding him, including the ones facing Illinois Avenue. Harry lucked out. One of his offers was accepted and he purchased the lot with our barn and driveway for about $100.

After getting petition signatures from supporters, fifteen angry, scrubby-looking hippies sat in the Land Bank's downtown lobby waiting for justice to be served. Land Bank officials knew they screwed up. But attempted mediation between all three parties left Harry secure in the knowledge that the property was now his.

Looking back, I don't resent Harry. He wanted the same opportunities to expand his backyard we did. Perhaps if I was a little wiser we could have mended the relationship, but we were young and idealistic and felt something we had earned through hard work was suddenly taken from us without just cause.

Afterward, the Land Bank, maybe fearing bad press, agreed to work with us on developing our project further, and over the next few months more than twenty overgrown house lots between Davison Road and Broadway Avenue were assembled as the Peace Mob Orchard. The massive six-acre site across Olive Avenue from the former Homedale Elementary School had all been demolished except for a couple of privately-owned structures facing Broadway Avenue or the old alley cutting the orchard in half. After receiving a $2,000 Maker grant from GOOD, we purchased plants for a permaculture food forest, we cleaned up fifty truckloads of trash, metal slag, and brush before planting in the hard clay ground. The orchard had forty-two fruit trees and twenty berry bushes. Branches were used as a natural trellis for eighteen grape vines along Davison Road. This space was a massive undertaking that could easily devolve into a four-foot-tall weed patch without regular maintenance. But by this time we had a fifty-year vision for expanding our self-sufficiency project and were confident it was attainable.

We adopted all the orchard lots and purchased our garden lots and the blue house next to Harry on Indiana Avenue from the Land Bank. Two other privately owned houses were purchased on Indiana and Illinois avenues. All of these properties as well as the pink house, were assembled as a housing co-op. The organization held the group's money, and each month "members" contributed towards shared bill payments and shared work around the various properties. This utopian system was debated over for months and by the time it was rolled out, the extensive contracts, bylaws, and regular meetings seemed adequate to cover any issues that could potentially arise.

A group of homesteaders pushed hard to make the project work. They set out, quickly making as many of the houses livable as possible while still experimenting in others with alternative ideas. In one house, the back southern wall was cut down to the studs and piecemealed into a greenhouse using brightly painted reclaimed wood windows. Shiny Mylar covered the interior walls to keep in heat and light. A single grow light hung above plywood shelves stacked with trays of vegetable sprouts cradled in newspaper diapers.

The house's water line to the street was broken, so the group jackhammered out the concrete slab in the house's basement and dug four-foot-deep cistern pits into the solid clay. Oily ground water would seep up and fill the pits. A sump pump moved water into a plastic trashcan that had a float switch spliced into the power plug to stop when it was full. A well pump bladder and PVC pipes then sent water from the trash cans upstairs to the toilet for flushing.

Another house's basement didn't have a furnace, so the group built a rocket stove and plenum. The clay- and sand-covered metal stove burned wood super efficiently, slowly radiating heat over hours and days. The problem was many of the people willing to participate in the social experiment and live on these troubled blocks tended to be low- or no-income, willing to work but unable to pay the bills. Or they were opportunists who could talk a big game but did no work. Despite mandatory monthly meetings and clear requirements to become worker-owners in the project, the division of labor became increasingly uneven and loaded on two elected individuals who managed the non-hierarchical organization.

As tensions and egos grew, the group branched off in several directions. Individual members transitioned into new stages of adulthood. Relationships ended and couples drifted away. Some members became parents suddenly. Some got steady jobs or started spinoff worker-owner businesses. Another moved into an army tent behind one of the houses before discovering his calling, working as a mechanic at

Burning Man.

The co-op officially launched July 4, 2012. Within two harsh winters, we were broke, demoralized and facing an unmanageable amount of taxes, shut-off notices, and unkempt properties. Without new blood, the massive project had reached its limits.

It was a cold winter when I finally left. My battered Cape Cod's blue vinyl siding was peeling like snakeskin, exposing the Styrofoam insulation underneath to the elements. The meticulously plastic-wrapped windows inside the home were stretched taut, fighting growing air gaps along the tapeline. The furnace had stopped sparking and I too was finally out of steam.

Moving out was a gut-wrenching admission of failure. But what we tried to do motivated others to follow similar paths around the time Peace Mob Gardens was falling apart. These other gardening and housing projects, led by expatriates who returned to Flint inspired by our efforts, have also struggled to survive over the past few years, but stand as examples for others wanting to try something crazy and utopian.

Within a season, neighbors had cleaned out the remaining garden tools, tomato cages, and anything metal that they could haul away. Other than Harry's manicured lawns, the properties remain vacant or overgrown like they were when we first moved in. They sit invitingly open, ready for the next group of dreamers trying to plant their freak flag and grow enough hope to nourish the whole neighborhood.

The Wild West on the East Side

STACIE SCHERMAN

A t 11:00 on a Saturday morning in July, my dad was rushing to his warehouse on the east side of Flint. He had just received a call from Greg, one of the neighboring business owners, that there were three teenagers breaking skylights on the roof of Dad's warehouse. Dad had already spent the previous three Mondays cleaning up broken glass from over 140 freshly broken windows, and he was anxious to confront the vandals. Despite Dad's normally healthy blood pressure (he tests it every chance he gets—at the drug store, gym, even at home—and sends me the latest results, giddy like he just made best score at his favorite game), it often spikes when he is stressed; even with his repeated reassurances that "I'm fine," I still worry. And now, Dad's blood pressure undoubtedly rose as he thought about the thousands of dollars in damage already caused in the warehouse, and the threat of much more if the kids got inside the building and further vandalized, burglarized, or worse.

Ten years prior he had made the same hurried drive in response to a call that the building was on fire. A homeless man had built a shelter out of several hundred pallets stacked up against the building. The structure was elaborately constructed and divided into two rooms; yet, located in the back of the building and obstructed by weeds, it was not easily accessible and even harder to see. From what my dad could see, the pallets were still a haphazard pile, just as they were when he bought the building, and the man was able to live in his pallet-home unnoticed for two months. Then, on one of the first cold nights of the fall, he started a fire in one of his pallet-rooms. The fire spread through the entire wooden structure, entering the warehouse through plywood that was bolted—ironically, for security protection— on both sides of the back windows. Once inside, the fire quickly moved through wall-to-wall, floor-to-ceiling rows of cardboard boxes, ultimately destroying a third of the building. Dad's insurance company used a loophole to avoid paying for the total damages, and the financial losses sent his business into a downward spiral that ended in Chapter thirteen bankruptcy.

This story is not surprising or uncommon in Flint. Arson is a particular threat on the east side, where abandoned, burned-out buildings checker the blocks in each direction; across the street from the warehouse, the front of an old brick building gapes open, revealing its charred remains. And in Flint, where the police may not even come when called (and the average response time to "high-priority crimes," at twenty-two minutes, is much higher than the national average), business owners and residents often revert to a state of nature, forming informal networks of alliance for crime prevention, surveillance, and response. "We watch out for each other," Dad often tells me, describing their actions as "self-policing."

As he drove now in pursuit of the teenage vandals, he thought about how quickly everything he built could be lost, having to start over yet again. After twenty-two years with the Grand Blanc Township Police Department, rising up from a patrol officer to captain, Dad was fired after a political disagreement with the new township supervisor. Dad sued the township supervisor for slander and won the case; he also sued Grand Blanc Township for wrongful discharge, and settled out of court. Yet the total financial award he received from both suits was only a fraction of the retirement pension he lost. At forty-four, and with a six-year-old daughter at home, he used his settlement to purchase a mini-storage business on the east side of the city. The potential to "be his own boss" attracted him to small-business ownership because of the control he thought it would provide over his own employment. Over the next ten years, he expanded his businesses to include a water trucking company; fiberglass pool sales, installation, and repair; and real estate investment, including condominiums, several commercial buildings, and the warehouse on Dort. All of which he lost in the bankruptcy, except for the Dort Highway warehouse.

After the fire, or the "crash and burn" as Dad describes it, he spent hours at the gym running in circles around the track—his only escape from the fallout both at work and at home. Dad first started running, several years before, so that he could spend time with me while I trained for and ran road races. But now I felt like the activity that once brought us together had turned into something that kept Dad away from home—and from me. I didn't understand then that almost everything he had built over the previous ten years literally went up in smoke, including the equity in his house. While his friends were reaching retirement age with mortgage-free homes, Dad was taking out a new mortgage—at the height of the housing bubble— that will likely not be paid off in his lifetime. Now, at sixty-eight, all he has left are the remaining 70,000 square feet of his warehouse, and he is resolved to protect all of it.

When Dad arrived, the kids were no longer visible from the street—they had squeezed through one of the newly broken windows, landing inside on stacks of boxes twenty feet off the floor. From the road, the old A&P grocery store and distribution center looks like just another run-down warehouse blending into the surrounding industrial decay. Its blue and red public warehouse sign is the only color that breaks up the grey monotony of its concrete exterior. Sheets of weathered plywood cover what used to be large windows, a battle long ago ceded to local teenagers with rocks and other projectiles. The building spans almost two acres and its flat roof enhances its already low profile. Sewage fumes creep up out of open grates in the parking lot and hang in the stagnant air, mixing with gasoline and fried food from across the street. On the far side of the warehouse, overgrown weeds and shrubs have reclaimed the land that once carried train cars to the now dusty and crumbling back loading dock. Cheap oil and impatience shifted transport from train to truck decades ago, leaving abandoned steel rail ties worth more in scrap than in use. Daily, semis lumber up the side road and sigh into an open dock, slowly turning pavement into gravel under their weight.

I took over the bookkeeping of Dad's business several years ago, and have since made weekly trips to the warehouse to pick up paperwork and bills, and drop off payroll checks. On one of my recent trips, sitting in the safety of my locked, climate-controlled car, I wondered what I was doing there, so far removed from the comforts of my own suburb. Then I remembered how painful it was, before I joined the business, to see Dad—exhausted after spending ten hours at the warehouse, coming home and staring at his computer, surrounded by stacks of papers, and struggling to sort through accounting forms and bookkeeping registers and bills. And so I know. As long as Dad is part of the warehouse (and the warehouse is part of him), I will be, too.

The only entrance into the building is through a metal door about four feet above the ground. There is no window or peephole, and the door is kept locked even during business hours; above the doorbell, rain-smeared ink on yellowed paper instructs visitors to "ring for service." When dad entered the building, he spotted the startled boys on top of the boxes and hollered at them to get down. One boy hesitated, appearing to consider Dad's order, before following his friends, who had already scrambled back through the broken window and onto the roof. They jumped down onto a lean-to, then onto some debris piled below on the back cement deck, and finally onto the ground, parkour style. Inside, Dad jogged across the warehouse floor and swung open the back door in time to see the kids dropping from the roof. He had left his Magnum in his truck, opting instead to bring a crowbar, more for intimidation than protection. "I just wanted to scare them," he told me.

Dad took off after the boys, already warmed up from his morning run. Dad likes to brag that he's in better shape than most men in their twenties, and he's probably right. Yet his wrinkles, receding and thinning hair, and weathered skin make him look all of his sixty-eight years. Dad often says that he wants his employees to know that he wouldn't ask them to do anything that he wouldn't do, but I wonder if it is really his way of proving that the old man can still keep up—like the time he unloaded 425 bags of rice, each weighing forty pounds, by hand while two twenty-somethings stood by and watched.

Outside, as the three boys ran, one lagged a few paces behind the other two—delayed by his hesitation inside the warehouse. Dad easily caught up to him first. Eyeing the crowbar and Dad's steely glare, the boy stopped running and begged, "Don't hit me don't hit me don't hit me!" Dad growled back, "Get down on the ground, and stay down." While the boy crouched, trembling, Dad continued his pursuit of the remaining two. Greg, Dad's neighbor, had been standing guard at the boys' getaway vehicles—three beat-up bicycles lying in the weeds next to the railroad tracks running through the back of the property. Now, as the boys ran, they found themselves sandwiched between the man with a crowbar and a slightly younger man in Carhartt overalls, my dad swiftly closing the gap.

Recognizing the futility of their escape, the two boys stopped running and surrendered. Dad slowed to a walk, unhurried but determined, and ordered the boys to walk back to the concrete deck, repeating the instructions to the first boy still cowering in the weeds. Dad and Greg then ushered all three inside the warehouse to wait for the police. For the next twenty minutes, Dad grilled them about the vandalism that had occurred over the previous three weeks, their roles, and who else was involved. One boy, who Dad describes as the "ringleader," maintained a tough façade and did most of the speaking, denying any involvement in the vandalism. The other two hung back, avoided eye contact, and said little, except to mumble that they had never been to the warehouse before that day. When the Flint police officer finally arrived, forty-five minutes after Dad's first call, all three boys immediately started crying—even the tough "ringleader." The officer asked a few questions, led the three boys to the cruiser, and drove them downtown.

When Dad tells me this story later that day, his eyes are bright, he is grinning widely, face animated, and he is cradling a fluffy white Maltipoo in his lap. It is hard to imagine this slight, gentle man, always laughing at his own (bad) puns, as the same intense, unyielding man in the story. But for Dad, confronting potential and actual vandals and burglars is just one of his job responsibilities, like unloading trucks and tracking inventory. He doesn't see himself as a hero, or special. He tells me that his "gun is just another tool," and that most of his employees and business neighbors carry the same "tools." The strangest part is how normal it is for Dad and his colleagues to chase bad guys, carry firearms, and hide weapons around (like crowbars) so that one is always within quick reach. "No one thinks anything of it, like back in the old west days. It's just the way it is."

A couple of days later, the mother of one of the teens—the one who had hesitated inside and begged Dad not to hit him—stopped by the warehouse to talk about her son. Outside the office, in the main part of the warehouse, forklifts zipped around with pallets stacked high with product; the warehouse manager inspected and marked large cardboard boxes waiting to be shipped out; semis idled in open loading docks. Yet inside the office, Dad did his best to make the mother feel comfortable, inviting her to sit down and giving her his complete attention, despite the activity going on just outside. The boy's mother wanted Dad to understand that the break-in and vandalism were not her son's normal behavior. His father had been murdered recently and he was having a difficult time coping. She said she kept a close watch on her son, but on the day of the vandalism he had lied about where he was going and who he was hanging out with. She promised that he would not be causing any more trouble at the warehouse.

Dad was impressed that the boy's mother came, unannounced, to the scene of her son's vandalism. He remembers thinking that it "took a lot of guts to walk in there not knowing what my reaction would be. Clearly she was concerned about her son." Dad told her that he didn't view her son with negativity; he was concerned about the material reality of repairing the existing property damage and preventing future destruction. He sympathized with her situation, but the case was out of his control at that point—he had already filed a crime report with the police and they were handling the investigation.

A couple of weeks later, Dad received a call from the probation office. As part of the procedure for processing this type of case, the probation office investigates all of the parties associated with the crime, including both suspects and victims, and prepares a pre-sentencing report. The investigation includes the victim's opinion of what should happen with the case; the probation officer who called Dad asked him specifically about restitution. The report is used to make recommendations to the prosecutor's office, and by the judge when deciding on sentencing.

Dad explained that if he had been adamant about wanting restitution, the probation office would strongly recommend that as part of the settlement of the case. But, he said, "What's restitution? You're looking at a $3000-$4000 loss. So the parents have to come up with the money? That doesn't serve any good purpose, us getting a check for a few bucks a month. These kids are obviously from a low income home, to take away money that the kids' families might have, I wouldn't feel good about it. They have a serious economic problem to begin with, this would just add to it."

A few months later Dad received a phone call from the probation office notifying him that the judge had decided to dismiss the case—no restitution, no probation. The representative calling had no other information, and Dad did not inquire further. He had little interest in the outcome of the case—his problem was already solved the day he caught the boys and knew they would not be back. Ultimately, in the state of nature of the east side, Dad's priority is protecting his livelihood and defending the small patch he has carved out in the city.

Before he hung up, Dad had already returned to his mental to-do list, deciding which "fire to put out" (ironically, one of his favorite phrases) next. He put his phone back in his pocket and disappeared into the rows of pallets and cardboard boxes.

Hyphen Flint

JAMES O'DEA

S he wanted to be gentle, but a philosopher does not hide the truth. "It's tough to get out of Flint," she told us. "You know it is."

The topic was graduate school, though her words stretched beyond that.

"It's the letterhead you have to overcome," she continued. This was not her usual seminar; this was more pressing than Hegel. She had to remind those who might forget: The Ivy Leagues don't want us, the blue-collar rabble of a -Flint school. The -Flint is an obscene addition, in their toplofty eyes, to the sanctified University of Michigan name. A heinous enough blasphemy to condemn even the most hopeful graduate school applications. She explained how we must market ourselves as exceptions to their rule, as -Flint students worth taking a chance on. Every letter of recommendation must be thoroughly convincing; every bullet-point on our resume must reassure them. We promise not to make you look bad. That is the only way to overcome the -Flint.

At conferences the -Flint on her nametag did not separate my professor from the intellectuals of richer schools. She was no less legitimate. But the condescending glances let her know who among her peers felt that way. As if teaching at a smaller, urban campus limited her prestige. The Ann Arbor tags have no dash. They simply say University of Michigan, implying that they are original and pure, not a spurious, hyphenated subspecies.

None of this should have been news to me. Flint is no stranger to stigma. The spotlight only finds our ugliest (and most marketable) sides: Violence. Crime. Poverty. Resources tainted by failing government and ailing infrastructure. But I was naïve enough at one time to believe the world of academia transcended petty biases. Instead my professor showed me academia's own unique breed of them. They were on display again when a close friend of mine—who published, tutored, ran student organizations, and helped design studies for the Flint Neurological Institute—was advised by another counselor not to waste money or effort attempting to get into any "Big Name" grad schools.

People spread horrific rumors of aborted opportunity, destinations where -Flint apps were guillotined on sight, tossed from the pile without hesitation. Their tales incited images of stuffy tweed-clad, elbow-patched men trashing -Flint applicants without a second sneer, refusing to hear a moment of their cases. If this is what it's like for us, I mourned for the Mott Community College students. Their -Flint bleeds deeper than the ink on our diplomas. Their -Flint is implied. Their school's name doesn't need the explicit -Flint disclaimer. It's already understood that their education is from the bargain bin. The name brand schools won't trust it. Community college is a -Flint unto itself.

Their talk reminded me of my suburban high school, how it saddened me to hear the disdain my classmates had for Flint. Mentioning Flint in a hallway of my school guaranteed at least one, "Don't get shot" or "Have fun in the ghetto!" Sure, I too was raised on dark jokes about crime rates and placement atop lists of America's most dangerous cities. But I could never look down on the city that made me.

When I told people I'd decided to go to U of M-Flint, their faces seemed to say, That's it? (Or, Poor thing, you have to stay home?) Nobody thought it was cool. Nobody congratulated me on getting in. Nobody got excited like they did for those going to Ann Arbor. I would overhear classmates justifying their -Flint: explaining that they'd be transferring after the first year, wanted to get their gen-eds out of the way, and how they would save a ton of money staying home. Although teachers assured me that U of M-Flint was a great school, I couldn't help sensing that a few of them had somehow expected better of me.

I didn't mind; I was too busy thinking too big for my idealistic britches, making declarations to revive Flint, lead a local literary revolution a la the Harlem Renaissance, and spur the city's return to glory. How writing poems was supposed to mollify Flint's post-industrial malaise was far beyond me. But it all sounded very cool at the time. My teachers usually responded somewhere between a grin and a chuckle—how one might react to a little boy promising to grow up to be an astronaut, a cowboy, and a dinosaur.

Those idyllic aspirations were quickly numbed and replaced once I started college. I discovered philosophy my first semester and spent the following years dreaming of what kind of professor I might be. I went from wanting to teach Joyce to wanting to be Wittgenstein. One semester I was going to teach law. Another it was philosophy of quantum physics. My longest affairs, however, were with philosophy of consciousness and creative writing. At graduation, I was looking into business school (a kick that lasted maybe three weeks). Never, though, did I stop seeking that gaudy resume, as had been inculcated in me to do so. And by the end of my tenure at the University of Michigan-Flint, I had it: publications, presentations, awards, and a flawless GPA. Following my professor's advice, I had made myself exceptional. And two years later, I have yet to attempt escape.

Truth is, I was never trapped here. My Irish ancestors have been a proud part of Flint since arriving in the early 1900s. In 1936, my great-grandfather—the first of four consecutive generations of James O'Deas—sat down in a factory not far from where I sit now, writing this with more gratitude than my words can carry. He sat for workers' rights. He sat in a strike that birthed the unionization that made blue-collar life viable. He sat so the dignity of common men might not be completely lost on those running the machines of power.

That is what I see when I see -Flint. My great-grandfather sitting on a dusty factory floor, my great-aunt Loretta bringing him a sandwich through the window. Sitting so I could sit in those classrooms. Sitting so his work and his son's work and his grandson's work could one day provide me the elusive opportunity of a higher education. Sitting so I could someday study philosophy, compose poetry, and thank him repeatedly in a graduation speech and in pieces like this one.

I see my father and grandfather parading through downtown on St. Patrick's Day, my brother and I behind them carrying a banner bearing our name and family crest. My -Flint is my inheritance, my history. I refuse to consider it a disability. I could not extricate myself from my -Flint if I tried. My name has been aligned with this city for over a century. I have no wish to wrench free of my historic roots.

But I am one of the lucky ones. I do not live in fear of escalating violence or rampant unemployment, though too many in our city do. I wake up in a bed with two dogs I love like children, in a room of book piles and wrestling mats for practicing jiu-jitsu, in a house shared with my brother and a close friend. Rent is cheap. Next door we help Barb, a retired teacher, carry in cases of water too heavy for her to lift. She struggles to hide the frustration with her weakening body, indomitable woman that she is, though I assure her it's our pleasure to help. I bartend enough to survive and buy local. The rest of my time is spent living simply, which for me involves a lot of poetry, dog hair removal, and stretching for jiu-jitsu. And there is nothing more I could ask for. I have found hidden in my hyperactive ambition the humble desire to live and write in a place that means something to me. Here, every day is an affirmation. My life is the fruit of my ancestor's labor, and I enjoy it wholeheartedly.

I still believe in revival, only I understand it better now. True progress is not made on the page or behind a microphone, though words can act as catalysts for change. Our lives are not led; they are grown. Same goes for an evolving city. And as I witness daily the seeds of future flourishing being sown, I want nothing more than to continue contributing in what small ways I can. Despite what setbacks befall us, our renaissance has begun. Which is why even in the face of tragedy I will always know without doubt: I am meant to be here. I do not want out.

Growing Up Eastside

MELISSA RICHARDSON

We grew up playing in the dust General Motors left behind. We proudly wore the dirt and grime of poverty on our faces, our clothes, our homes, and let it leave its mark on our lives. We were rough and tough. Disadvantaged, because we knew that the world just wouldn't have enough sandpaper to smooth out all of our edges. We knew all the cuss words and how to enunciate them with gusto, before learning to say "please" and "thank you." We were on the tail end of a once great educational system that was in steep decline and embedded with controversy and financial woes. But no matter the grades we made and the training the world afforded, we would always hold on affectionately to our gritty spots, our misplaced cuss words, our inappropriate slips of slang or the Flint town swagger that we just couldn't shake.

We grew up as the grandchildren of the "Last Great Generation." Our forefathers were the ones who walked right out of high school and onto the production floor at General Motors. They were our goliaths, easing into their retirement just as General Motors was shipping their jobs overseas. Our parents were left to scavenge for scraps of jobs and stand in long welfare lines. They became useless and resentful of the world, of us. We coped by turning our parents into small images in the background of our lives. We had no idea that our futures were dark and scary.

We were instantly associated with Franklin Avenue, Kearsley Park, Luigi's, Amus Park, and whether or not you were a Homedale Hornet or Washington Wildcat. Proximity to these locations determined your depth of "eastsidedness"; the closer you were, the more authentic of an eastsider you were. If you lived east of Dort Highway and north of Richfield Rd. or south of Court St. you might as well have claimed another side of Flint, you just didn't count. You trimmed your grass bi-weekly, painted and repaired your homes when necessary and more often than not, never left a broken down car in your driveway to rust away through the elements.

Your neighborhood was just too nice.

We grew up eastsiders, which meant that most of the time, we were merely surviving. It meant that our clothes were secondhand, and not the nice consignment store secondhand. They were either worn and torn hand-me-downs from an older sibling or a lucky find from the dollar bag day at St. Vincent de Paul's on Franklin Ave. Our baby brother or sister often ran around outside in just their diaper and a dirty pacifier, parents dismissive about sunscreen, hand sanitizer, or heat exhaustion. We were often neglected, more often than not tossed to the side, like an afterthought.

Eastsiders took pride in the little things, because sometimes that was all that we had. One summer, we felt like the luckiest kids in the world when they repaved Decker St. The project took four days to complete and we all waited in bated anticipation on the corner of Roosevelt Ave. and Decker St. for it to be completed. We had never seen a street repavement up close and personal. The large machines, the smell of fresh, hot asphalt, and the sight of the overheated men were the topics of our conversations, morning and night. At one point we all had determined that we wanted to be street construction workers when we grew up. To us, those four days felt like four months. And then one morning we woke up to the trucks and workers gone and in their place a smooth, glasslike, black asphalt surface that stretched the span of two whole city blocks. Without even saying a word, we all raced home and grabbed our skates or bikes. That summer, the City of Flint gave us the best gift ever; we had never skated on such a smooth surface outside of a gymnasium or skating rink. For those who didn't have skates, we took turns with one another's. For those who had a bike, we offered to pull the skaters behind the bikes while they held onto the seat, weaving them from left to right at a dangerous pace, unaware of the consequences. The new Decker St. asphalt became our playground that summer, our playtime only to be temporarily halted by passing cars.

We grew up in our own little world, comfortably nestled between Robert T. Longway, Interstate 475, and Kearsley Park. My eastside was cut off from the rest of the world. On a good night, over the southwestern horizon you could see the hazy, neon light pollution from downtown, blocking out the stars and obscuring the night sky. We only vaguely knew that just over the interstate catwalk was an unknown history and the remnants of a once "great city" that was unbeknownst to us, rapidly crumbling.

My eastside was Kearsley Park. To others it was just another place in Flint that was a dilapidated shadow of its former glory. The few playground toys that remained on the southwest side of the park were rusty, half-,broken or in complete disarray. From within the tall grass, you could see the remains of "Safety Ville, U.S.A." In its heyday it was a public go-cart track that taught our parents about motor safety as children. We only knew of its existence from our parents' stories. To us it was broken pieces of asphalt, deteriorating structures, and rusted metal that protruded from the ground in obscene and foreboding ways. At the top of the southeast hill stood the park's pavilion. The pavilion was off-limits; even after multiple "Operation Brush-Up" attempts it was perpetually covered in gang signs, broken glass, and the distinct smell of human piss.

We grew up with a park that was less than welcoming to the stranger, often perceived and at times proven, as dangerous as it was rumored to be. We grew up having no idea that non-eastsiders called Kearsley Park "Dark Park" because at night it only had one functioning light, which made it unsafe to travel through once the sun had set. We didn't know that the gang signs and broken glass that covered the pavilion were indications that the Spanish Cobras frequently used the location as a hangout at night, where they would party with their fellow gang members, blasting Chicago house music and initiating new gang members by beating them within an inch of their life. We didn't know that the toys we climbed and played on during the day housed homeless vagrants during the night, seeking shelter, solitude, and a good night's rest. We grew up only knowing what the sun could touch. We knew enough to stay away from the darkness.

Kearsley Park was our diamond in the rough and tough concrete jungle that was Flint. Its only saving grace was its enormity and its natural beauty. The park was flanked by tree lines and rolling hills, with a small creek cutting right through its very heart. The tree lines housed our forts, hide-and-go-seek games, and some of the best sledding trails for the courageous and oblivious youth. In the spring we ran up the hills only to throw our bodies down at the top and roll down to the bottom. We spent our winter afternoons sledding down, running home for a quick "warm up" of hot cocoa on subzero days. But the best times had at the park were in the summer, after a good hard rain had flooded the ground with an inch or two of Kearsley Creek.

My eastside existed in the simplicity of gathering the neighborhood kids for a game of football, baseball, street hockey, or hide-and-go-seek. One day, early into a well-deserved summer break, we ventured into a game of football of epic proportions. It had rained nice and hard the night before and the park, in its usual fashion, had flooded. We stood at the top of the hill, next to my home and looked down at the creeping water when one of us came up with a grand scheme that we knew would either be legendary or disastrous. We decided to try to play football at the park and in the water at the bottom of the hills behind our homes. There was no hesitation, even from the weakest links; everyone was in agreement. We ran home to put on our worst clothes to avoid getting a good smack upside the head later when we returned home covered in mud and creek water. Barreling down the trails through the woods, we all met at the bottom of the hills on the southwest side of the creek. The eastside kids from the Kearsley Park neighborhood abandoned their usual game of one- or two-hand touch football and played tackle football that day, recklessly slamming each other into the muddy Flint tributary, sending up great splashes and waves all around us. We ran, we dove, we tackled and we fell all over the place. All the while knowing that we would never be able to recreate these moments ever again, even down to seeing our parents' own looks of disbelief when we showed up at the door sopping wet and smelling slightly musty, to washing earthworms from our hair and mud from our ears later on that day.

My eastside was Angelo's Coney Island on the corner of Davison and Franklin Ave., a small restaurant that had become famous for its Flint-style coney dogs. Eastsiders knew too well the overpowering aroma of an Angelo's coney dog wafting down Franklin Ave. on a good windy day. Angelo's was the only place that you got to become familiar and up and close with the legendary, delectable, and familiar snap of a Koegels-brand Vienna dog nestled in a softly steamed bun, smothered in mustard and onion, and overflowing with the top-secret Angelo's coney sauce. Flint-style coney was the only coney you knew (Detroit was nonexistent) and the only way you knew that made a hot dog so damn good. Eastsiders overlooked Angelo's dismal appearance, with its heavily outdated and equally worn out decor. We did not notice or mind the florescent lightbulbs, brownish-green linoleum, stainless steel bar top, and faded Formica topped tables amidst a backdrop of crumbling and peeling yellowish-brown wallpaper that was covered with pictures and articles of Flint's own hero: the one-armed pitcher, Jim Abbott. We carefully maneuvered the floors that were heavily laden with grease and soot, that often made a trip to your favorite booth an adventurous game of slip and slide. The vinyl booths were cracked and peeling, bar stools had exposed stuffing or showed attempts of repair with heavy duty duct-tape. We felt at home among the familiar sight of the tables and counters that were adorned with genuine glass Heinz 57 bottles, steel napkin dispensers, and the novelty tiny jelly packet holders.

My eastside was a neighborhood that openly welcomed everyone, regardless of race, creed, or religion, even at a time when Flint was rumored to be the most segregated city this side of the Mason-Dixon Line. We had two Mexican families, a Hungarian family, and two interracial families that lived just on our block. Poverty on the eastside knew no boundaries and drew no lines. We grew up without cliques and we all had friends of more than just one race or ethnicity. Our only prerequisite was that you were poor—and if you lived in our neighborhood that was a given.

We grew up walking our streets, riding our bikes, skating on the pavement freely. We moved from block to block with no concern, no worry, no fear, and no hesitation. We walked to the party stores and bought penny candy, twenty ounces of Big K, packets of Limón Sevens, and bags of Doritos with our allowances, lawn-mowing money, or our parents' food stamps. We walked to Heddy's Market with notes in our hands and left with packs of cigarettes and forty ounces of beer for our parents and grandparents. Donna, the svelte but manly owner of Heddy's Market, would be standing outside watering her flowers or talking to a passer-by between customers. She would say "hi" and call to you by name. She knew you, she knew your parents, and she also knew that your parents had a growing credit bill with her store that made her wonder if maybe she had been a little too generous last month. Regardless of what your parents owed her, she would still sponsor next season's Little League team and under her guidance, the team remained undefeated. You knew to never try to steal from Heddy's Market, not out of fear of being caught and punished by your parents but mostly out of fear of disappointing Donna. Your parents and their mounting debts and excuses had done that enough already. We knew no different and no one looked at us differently, as long as we stayed on our own little side of Flint.

I am now grown and never realized that eventually when I would tell people I am from Flint with a hint of pride in my voice, they would look at me in surprise and exclaim, "I would have never guessed you grew up in Flint!" I did not know that while they silently took stock of my fair skin, blue eyes, and then-blonde hair and tried to place me, in their mental context, as a child growing up on the eastside of Flint, I would feel a creeping sense of shame. I would have never guessed that sometimes they would go so far as to visibly take steps away from me, as to physically distance themselves from anything associated with Flint. I did not realize that some people were scared that too much association or contact with me might cause a little bit of "my Flintness" to rub off on them. Or that a slip of slang or use of incorrect grammar here and there would be instantly attributed to someone telling me that "your Flint is showing." I never realized that outsiders, being void of any understanding of my past and my memories, would view Flint and anything associated with it as unsafe.

There is no denying it, no way to sugarcoat it even, and taking a drive through my eastside is heartbreaking, scary, and despairing to most. Outsiders would caution themselves, roll up their windows, and make sure their doors are locked before driving down Franklin Ave. An outsider would stare in disbelief that such a place even exists, let alone is even inhabited by fellow humans. The eastside that they see is not the eastside that I see, that I know. What I see is strength, resiliency, and determination from these places. These places, like their residents, have endured the test of time and still manage to stand. Kearsley Park has been restored to a small semblance of its former glory, before the gangs and poverty wreaked havoc and scarred its face. The park has been cleaned up and regularly maintained. It now hosts "Shakespeare in the Park" and Mott Community College ball games. The reality of depleting funding and support only reinforce that, as always in Flint, all good things must come to an end. That is unless you are Angelo's. An eastside landmark, its original location still stands, even after having undergone multiple owners, franchising failures, and changes to its "secret sauce" that drove away loyal customers, only to bring them back again after it stopped trying to change and accepted itself for what it was: eastside.

What's taken the biggest hit are our neighborhoods. Yes, they are comparable to war zones or a ghost town. Most homes are abandoned, boarded up, fallen in disrepair, burned up, or razed to the ground. Vacant, overgrown lots remain in their place. But what I see is that parts of our neighborhoods still stand. Homes that look inhospitable at first glance, with broken windows, busted porch steps, and peeling paint jobs, still have signs of life. There are cars in the driveway, children standing on the front porch, disregarded toys and trash litter their yards. These silent visual reminders tell me that the eastside has not been abandoned and, in its usual "dirty" type of way, it refuses to be forgotten.

These memories are my eastside, they are me. Each one defined my palette, my character and my imagination. Each memory challenges me with what I saw, what I did and what I allowed myself to think I could grow up and do. I am now grown but I have not forgotten my roots; rather, they won't let me forget about them. Very often when working on a task or deep in my own thoughts, I am asked by complete strangers, "Are you okay?" or asked to "Smile!" while they exclaim "It can't be that bad!" I am told by strangers and familiar faces that I look "mean" and "unapproachable." In moments like this I laugh it off on the outside, subduing their fears and putting them at ease by revealing my sanded-down edges, but I smile on the inside because it's these moments that remind me that no matter how "soft" I become with my college education and suburban home, my eastside is and always will be showing.

Meet the Flintstones

EDWARD MCCLELLAND

Note: Originally published in The Morning News.

The 9/11 Memorial Corner occupies three of the four lots at the intersection of North and McClellan streets, on the vanishing north end of Flint. A cross between folk art and patriotic kitsch, its backdrop is a pentaptych of the Manhattan skyline, with the Twin Towers still the tallest stalks in that architectural garden. A ceramic angel spreads her plaster wings atop the middle panel, while in the grass — more tightly barbered here than in any of the surrounding yards — is a statuette of the Virgin Mary bowing her head. Written on a billboard are the names of every police officer and firefighter who died that Tuesday morning. A winding path of cinder blocks bears a hand-painted roll call of all the soldiers who never came home from Afghanistan. "OUR (heart) AND (praying hands) GO OUT TO THE WORLD. GOD BLESS 9-11-01 AMERICA," reads the message on a concrete foundation road-mapped with weeds.

I discovered the corner six years ago, while searching for the remains of Buick City, a factory that once employed 28,000 autoworkers before it closed in 1999, leaving behind a neighborhood of shuttered taverns, party stores, stringy people sitting on slanted porches, and a Realtor's sign planted on the front lawn of UAW Local 599 headquarters. There are 12,000 vacant residential lots in Flint, and the corner occupies three of them. I wasn't walking long among its roster of the dead before a small, tattooed woman appeared on the porch of one of the block's three remaining houses and crossed the street.

Suzie Fitch curated the site, checking the Internet every day for deaths of American soldiers in Afghanistan, recording the sad news with a fine-tipped brush. When an Army psychiatrist killed thirteen military personnel at Fort Hood, Texas, in 2009, Suzie filled an unused lot with wooden blocks bearing the names of each victim.

"We just lost two this weekend," she said. "We lost forty-seven in April."

"What about the soldiers in Iraq?" I asked.

"Iraq didn't have nothin' to do with 9/11," Suzie said. "I can't wait until the war is over. I wish we never gone into Iraq. We should finish Afghanistan first. We had to go there, no ifs, ands or buts. They're the ones who killed us."

A pickup truck pulled up across the street. Suzie's husband, Moose, home from hanging drywall, walked over to join us. Moose wore a ponytail, a graying beard, and a T-shirt with the face of a similarly bearded man then still at large in the Middle East. "WANTED," it read. "OSAMA BIN LADEN."

Before the Fitches built their memorial, "the neighborhood was using that corner as a public dump site," Moose said. "We still find a lot of stuff down there. You get tired of looking at garbage because people just don't care. They don't take the pride in their country that I saw as a child."

Moose and Suzie had met in Chicago, her hometown, then returned to Flint, his hometown, because he needed to be close to his children by an earlier marriage.

"When he brought me here, he's like, 'Wait till you see Flint,' she said. "'It's happening. It's goin' on. It's a mini Chicago.' And I come here and I'm like...."

"I was embarrassed," Moose confessed. "The whole time I was gone, it went to hell."

"We're gettin' out of here," Suzie said. Then she jumped in the air and stamped on the sidewalk. "I am not gonna die in Flint, Michigan!"

After that encounter, I stopped at the 9/11 Memorial Corner every time I was in Flint. I wrote about the corner in my Rust Belt history, *Nothin' but Blue Skies: The Heyday, Hard Times and Hopes of America's Industrial Heartland*, and continued visiting after the book came out, because I considered Moose and Suzie friends, and because the corner is my favorite Flint tourist attraction. I'm not the only one. On Memorial Day 2011, I attended a candlelight vigil. The bikers arrived first, a gray-haired iron cavalry called the Christian Motorcyclists Association of America. Their "Riding for the Son" vests were embroidered with Indian arrowheads—Flint's civic emblem—identifying them as the Flint Area Good News Riders.

Moose, who is patriotic without being political, wore a T-shirt that read, "I SUPPORT MY COUNTRY AND OUR TROOPS. PRAYER FOR THE PRISONERS AND MISSING." He had strung fleece Marine Corps blankets along a wire, lit candles inside glowing cutaway milk jugs, set up a video camera on a tripod, and was now walking along the improvised plank benches and folding chairs, recruiting veterans to fold the flag. (Moose has never served in the military himself, which may be why he so admires veterans.)

When the audience numbered three dozen—a good crowd for an outdoor vespers, which is what the ceremony in the long late-spring Michigan evening felt like—Moose made a speech.

"Will all the veterans stand up? We're here to honor the fallen veterans, the veterans still fighting, and the families. We need to start supporting our veterans, because they give us the freedom to do this."

Even in late May, Michigan sunlight doesn't last forever. It mellows and dissolves. As the infiltrating darkness grayed the evening beyond the balance point between day and night, Suzie laid lilies at a wooden cutout of a soldier's silhouette, then read a poem clipped from a newspaper. ("Memorial Day is a day of tears / For those who died over the years.") Finally, she led the congregation across the street to her memorial and asked everyone to recite, in unison, a name she'd painted atop a cinder block. In the vigil's final act, the names of three dozen dead soldiers, sailors, and airmen overlapped each other.

The 9/11 Memorial Corner could not exist anywhere but a city like Flint. Where else could the Fitches have acquired as much vacant land for their patriotic crèche? As the houses surrounding Buick City emptied out, the Fitches bought up vacant lots from the Genesee County Land Bank, which sold them for as little as $25 to neighbors willing to cut the grass.

The couple had expanded their yard nearly to the end of the block. The only corner they didn't own was squatted on by a dead-eyed house that had become a dumping ground for old mattresses; it remained upright only because the city couldn't afford to bulldoze it. The Fitches didn't own the land across the street, but Moose mowed the lawns anyway, so drug dealers couldn't hide their stashes in the weeds. One hundred years after GM's founding, Flint is at the far end of its historic arc. The Vehicle City had been built to produce automobiles, but since the plants wore out it is being disassembled at the same geometric rate at which it had risen. In the damp, lush climate of Lower Michigan, verdure is relentless, crawling through every sidewalk fault, packing every empty space with thick grass. Red clover, teasel, yarrow, and toadflax have forced themselves through the concrete slabs that once supported Buick City and Chevy in the Hole, another demolished auto plant. Trees encroach on the yards Moose tries to keep clear—trees broad enough for drugs dealers to hide themselves behind. Carl Sandburg's poem "Grass" seems appropriate for the Memorial Corner, since it's about war dead. "Two years, ten years, and passengers ask the conductor: / what place is this? / where are we now / I am the grass. / Let me work." But it's also appropriate for Flint itself, disappearing under vegetation.

Moose is fifty-seven years old now. Hanging drywall has left him with bone spurs on his spine, arthritis in his joints. Allergic to pain medication, he has no choice but to endure the aches that are his trade's only pension. Last winter, the Michigan cold caused him "a massive amount of pain." So much pain that he decided to leave Flint, for Roswell, New Mexico, where he knows a Mormon missionary who visited the corner while evangelizing in the Vehicle City years ago.

"A lot of people say warm weather will help me," Moose said. "I'll be young enough to start a new life. I'm going to try to do something where I don't have so much lifting."

Moose figured they needed $3,500 to make it to New Mexico. That would be enough to fix up his 1991 GMC Safari for the 1,500-mile drive, and rent him and Suzie an apartment until they could find jobs. He had a check coming from a drywall job that would finance the move.

Moose and Suzie could have raised enough money by selling their house. Flint has the lowest housing prices in the United States—an average of $15,000. It's not just that ninety percent of the auto industry jobs are gone, and that Flint is among the most violent cities in the English-speaking world, with a murder rate of sixty per 100,000 in 2013, equal to Latin American drug capitals. It's that 21st-century Americans don't want to live in the workingman's specials Flint threw up to house the Michigan dirt farmers, Ozark mountaineers, and African-American sharecroppers who flooded the city in the 1920s and 1930s to build Buicks and Chevys. Moose's house is three bedrooms, 900 square feet, full bath up, half bath down. Now, everyone wants a house on two acres in the suburbs, or a loft in The Durant, downtown Flint's faded glory hotel, recently converted to luxury apartments. Moose's house is a mid-size dwelling for a middle-class city, which Flint hasn't been since the early 1980s, when General Motors began withdrawing from its hometown. In 1980, when a young man could still walk out of high school and into an auto plant, Flint had the highest median income for workers under thirty-five in the nation. Since then, that figure has fallen forty percent, more than any other city. Today, the median household income is $41,249.

The house would have fetched $25,000, Moose figured. But if he sold it, would the new buyer look after the 9/11 Corner? He couldn't make that a condition of the sale price. So Moose decided to give away his house, along with the condition that the new owners tend the corner.

"Being poor like we are, we're going to be poor here, or we're going to be poor somewhere else," he figured. "It's a leg up for someone."

Another reason Moose was eager to find new occupants: in Flint, empty houses are stripped of copper piping, plumbing fixtures, chain-link fences, and any other metal that desperate scavengers can sell down at the scrap yard, as they try to salvage every last nickel of wealth remaining in the city. It's not unknown for scavengers to carry boilers down the street in broad daylight. The police don't stop them. They've got deeper shit to deal with. A few years ago, the mayor laid off a third of the force, and now it takes the cops fifty minutes to respond to a shooting. That's one reason why Flint has so many murders. If you have fifty minutes to get away, what's the deterrent?

Maybe Moose was naïve to think that he could spare his corner from the forces of decay that have overtaken the rest of the north end. As the saying goes, "Nature always bats last." Moose had been naïve before. Sincere and transparent, he projects those qualities onto everyone he meets.

In 2004, Moose appeared in Michael Moore's anti-Iraq War film, *Fahrenheit 9/11*, after the filmmaker discovered the 9/11 Memorial Corner on a hometown visit. Moose didn't know Moore from D.W. Griffith, but he'll show off his corner to anyone, so he allowed the director to film them driving around the north end in Moose's pickup.

"They said they were taking pictures of memorials to 9/11, and the movie was going to be about honoring those folks of 9/11," Moose told me later. "He came up to my wife: 'This is the best thing we've seen in the city of Flint.'"

Once the movie came out, though, Moose felt he'd been a victim of journalistic trickery. This was Moose's quote, as it appeared in *Fahrenheit 9/11*: "Look at the neighborhood I live in. Most of 'em are abandoned. That's not right. You want to talk about terrorism? Come right here. President Bush, right here. He knows about this corner."

Moose's words give the impression that he was blaming gangbangers for terrorizing the north end. In fact, Moose said, Moore combined two unrelated quotes. The second half was a response to the question, "Who do you want to visit this corner?"

As a result of his *Fahrenheit 9/11* appearance, Moose was tracked down by another Flint documentarian: Kevin Leffler, producer of *Shooting Michael Moore*, a muckraking exposé on America's No. 1 muckraking exposer.

In the film, Moose tearfully demands to know how Moore could misrepresent his patriotic display. There is no cynicism or irony at the corner of North and McClellan, and Moose seems hurt that a Hollywood director could introduce such notions into his carefully tended garden of Americana.

"Mr. Moore," he says, his voice welling, "how can you do this when you say you love this country and you talk for the small man? Mr. Moore, you broke our heart, just like 9/11 broke this country's heart."

Moose gets emotional over two subjects—America and his wife. In his mind, Moore had violated both.

At first, Moose tried to give his house to a soldier. He went to a Veterans Administration hospital and a Veterans of Foreign Wars Hall, but in both places he got the same reaction. The north end? That's the most violent drug marketplace in Flint. He offered the house to a member of the Flint Area Good News Riders, the Christian motorcyclists group that attends Memorial Day candlelight vigils at the corner. They didn't want it, either.

"Because of the violence and all the hatred, it's been very hard," Moose said. "Everybody basically said they don't want to live here because of what's here. But it's peaceful compared to what it was. When we moved in here nineteen years ago, the news people reported on drug deals. They talked about it being a curbside drug market. But now all the properties around here are clear, so someone can come in and build the life they want."

By June, having failed in three attempts to give away his house, Moose thought about a young man who'd grown up in the north end, just a block away from the corner. Moose had known Jevon since he was eight or nine. One day, he was packing his poles in the truck to go fishing. A bunch of neighborhood kids saw him, and asked to go along.

"I took 'em out fishing, and every one of 'em caught a fish but me," he recalled.

(I found out about Moose's plans to give away his house when he called me last month. Nowadays, most people keep in touch by e-mailing or leaving curt messages on Facebook, but Moose still calls people. Usually, he calls me on holidays— Thanksgiving, Memorial Day, the Fourth of July—but this time he called just to say hello and tell me to "give hugs and kisses" to my three-month-old daughter.)

When Moose and Suzie were building the memorial, Jevon traced an outline of the New York City skyline on the platform in front of the mural. Jevon was married now, with a six-year-old daughter and a four-month-old son. But the young family was too poor to afford its own place. Jevon sometimes earned money doing manual labor, such as tearing down trailers, but he was unemployed now. His wife, Cassidy, worked twenty hours a week at McDonald's, earning $8.47 an hour. So they bounced around between relatives. They'd lived with Jevon's mom, on the north end. Now they were staying with Cassidy's mother, on the east side of Flint. Moose called him.

"Hey, young man," he asked. "How'd you like your own house?"

Jevon said he'd have to talk it over with his wife. When he did, Cassidy was speechless. The north end didn't scare them, because they'd lived there before. And they'd only have to pay $133 a month in property taxes.

"Not being able to afford our own place, we've kind of been going by as we go," Cassidy told me when Moose set up a three-way call between us. "This means everything to us. It's just so hard trying to do everything by myself, 'cause I'm the only one working."

There is only one stipulation: Jevon and Cassidy have to mow the grass on the corner. Moose is going to continue paying property taxes on the corner's three lots, until he can find someone who will continue adding the names of soldiers killed in Afghanistan.

Moose is planning one final candlelight vigil, for July 11. On that evening, he'll announce that he and Suzie are leaving Flint for New Mexico, and introduce Jevon and Cassidy to his regular band of patriots. A few days later, if all goes according to plan, he'll head for the Sun Belt. It's a journey thousands of Flintstones have made before. Flint's population is half what it was in 1960, when it topped out at 196,000. But unlike so many of the migrants who preceded him, his place in Flint won't be filled by blight or weeds.

"I'm obviously going to mow it," Cassidy said of the corner. "I haven't really decided beyond that. We'll go as it goes."

A Boy and His Graveyard:

Resurrecting the History and Mysteries of Glenwood Cemetery

SARAH MITCHELL

A boy named Peter visits a cemetery. He didn't visit to seek a scare or to vandalize, as many kids do, but because multiple generations of his family had been buried there. His ancestors had come to Flint in the 1850s, the very decade Glenwood Cemetery was founded. The iron fence, an army of finial-topped bars, secures the perimeter, but the gates are open, welcoming him and his family as they pass through. Just inside, to the left, stands the old house of the caretaker. Shutter-flanked windows cover the structure's two stories, and on the side facing the entrance, one of two chimneys peeks shyly from the angular roof to greet Glenwood's guests.

Beyond the house, the path splits. To the left, it descends steeply into a valley—likely one of the glens that inspired the cemetery's name—and shortly before reaching the bottom, forks to create the mouth of a long loop. The paths converge on a hill in the middle of this small wing of the cemetery. To the right the path takes a gentler slope through a dense thicket of headstones, monuments, and mausoleums leading guests towards the heart of Glenwood. The boy goes with his family to the right.

They head down the path to visit their ancestors, the Atwoods, whose members include people once active in Flint's public and political spheres and whose name is still recognizable in the city. The boy's grandfather—and several great-grandparents before him—rest here. He's learning what it means to respect those who've passed and the past they represent, but he's still young. As he honors his own relatives, he can't know the significance of where he stands, surrounded by some of Flint's most prominent citizens and thousands more that played their own little part—no matter how thankless—in building the city. There, in that rolling forest of etched granite, limestone, and marble, he has no way of knowing what this place will come to mean to him and what it already means to Flint.

It is the mid-1850s. Genesee County commerce is burgeoning. The local lumber industry is on the rise. Land is cheap, and people are flocking. Newspapers are flying off the press. Businesses are opening. Money is becoming a reality. And Flint is the hub of it all.

A group of men are thinking. Maybe an offhand remark sparked the idea, some conversation ignited by someone's trip to a big city in the east or by the mouth of a newcomer. They know what's happening around town. They watched as the population of this village and its outlying communities expanded, and noted their own accounts swelling right along with the tide. There's word that, any day now, Flint will finally be incorporated as a full-fledged city. A few decades ago, this place was little more than a tiny village with a trading post started by a fur trader—one with the rather generic name of Jacob Smith—and his Ojibwa wife. Innumerable trees, acres upon acres of unsettled land, the river, and some Ojibwa villages were about all the area had to offer. But that was the ancient past as far as these men are concerned. They agree. It's time to find a tract of land. There's plenty of land around, of course, but it can't be just any old plot. No, they're looking for something specific.

Romanticism, with its occasional tinges of Gothic melancholy and intense focus on nature and emotion, has had its way in the realm of art and literature. Around the turn of the century, the movement materialized in the practical world as beautifully landscaped properties and cemeteries. Born in Europe and sweeping east to west across the United States, it has finally reached Flint. They need property fit for a sanctuary, a park. So, they set out, determined to find a place of beauty, somewhere that would accommodate the needs and desires of the surging population, a place to properly honor the dead.

Years have passed by and that boy is now a young man. He still visits Glenwood, but boyish musings have given way to more mature thoughts and actions. He's begun to appreciate beauty, history, life—and its end—in a way that only age can bring. There is a girl now, of course. She understands and shares his love for the unique kinds of splendor found in nature and history. And so they go walking. From time to time, they find themselves strolling down the same paths he took as a child. The context has changed, but the place is the same. The headstones and monuments are ever aging. The land is still rolling and wooded—an unframed, romantic landscape. On breezy spring and summer days, the peace allows the wanderers to hear the wind tickling the leaves of the ancient guardians, who, come autumn, knit their foliage into a variegated afghan of orange, red, and yellow, tucking in their charges in preparation for winter. The couple's light footfalls and conversation pepper the quietude. They are there, as the man would say years later, to "drink it in."

The men have surveyed the whole of Flint. It's taken some time to find the right spot. This has been in the works for a couple of years. They've looked over tract after tract, but one, in particular, stands out. It has the mix of space—a must—and aesthetics that they're looking for. To the north, it's bounded by the Flint River, to the east and west, wooded ravines. Very little of the property is level. This may present some challenges when it comes to interments and erecting monuments, but the beauty of it is well worth the slight risk of inconvenience. This particular property comes with the added bonus of having once been a part of the holdings of Jacob Smith, the man credited with first settling the area—or at least the first white man to do so. It is, in that way, important in its own right. And these men believe they're doing something important too.

The stockholders are all prepared to put in their share. It's settled. This picturesque property will be the new home of Glenwood Cemetery. It will be the only cemetery of this caliber in the area. Simple proficiency is out; ornamentation is in. The county has finally reached the point that fashion can take a little precedence over mere function. After all, much of America has already moved away from cramped churchyards and plain rows of burials, creating instead peaceful, nature-cradled retreats to honor those who slumber and comfort those that do not. Once the cemetery is open, citizens will have a proper place for meditating, meandering, mourning. The men are hoping to have the property prepared within a handful of months. Now is the time to work. Books need to be kept. Plans need to be drawn up. The word needs to be spread. Hard work got Flint to this point, and it will eventually raise Glenwood up too.

The days of boyhood have long since passed, and the young man had to navigate life—even as he periodically visited the dead. He chose an occupation. Finance and accounting seemed to suit him, so he went with that. And he married that girl along the way, too. He never lost his appreciation for what the cemetery is—this resting place of his ancestors and a place of natural beauty. No matter what changed in his life, Glenwood stayed essentially the same. Time seems slower here. Every once in a while, if only fleetingly, he wonders what it would be like to live there—not as a permanent resident, of course, but as the caretaker. It seems an unusual job, but an interesting one. He wonders what it entails. Is it only the opening and closing of the gates? How does a person even get that job? Who makes the decision to hire some-one? What kind of person does it take?

They're only a few passing thoughts, though. That's all.

It's October of 1857. The time has finally come. The grounds are prepared and have been sectioned off into lots and plots. A dedication has been planned. Several local pastors have agreed to handle the service. Rankin, the editor of the weekly Flint-based paper, *The Wolverine Citizen*, has been contacted. The work now done, the ambitious men can only wait, hope, and pray that their vision is shared by the populace. People from all over the county will see the article outlining the day's events. Lots will be for sale immediately after the ceremony is concluded. These men, the stockholders, know that they want spots for themselves and their fami-lies, but wonder if other people care enough to follow suit. Death is inevitable, but there are other places that could be chosen instead. They aren't like this one, of course—the romantic terrain, winding pathways, artistic design, but does that mat-ter enough? Will people choose Glenwood? The excitement of potential success and the apprehension of a lukewarm reception battle for dominance in their minds.

Our young man, who may by now be referred to as simply a man, has found him-self at a brokerage firm—Roney & Co. This isn't exactly monumental news, but perhaps, there is more here than it seems. There among the various accounts lies the name of a certain cemetery. Cemeteries, after all, have books that need to be kept. The original proprietors, having long ago taken up residence themselves, can no longer handle them. It seems that he can't help but be intertwined with Glenwood—first by family urging, then by choice, and now, seemingly, by chance, or maybe by design. As he serves the cemetery on a pro bono basis, he learns the inner workings, the expenditures and the revenue.

Then, in 2008, the offer came.

The regal, solemn, but celebratory sound of the Flint Brass Band is ringing out as the congregation starts to sing the hymn "Old Hundred." It's a little past 10 o'clock on the morning of Wednesday, October 28th. A few minutes ago, a prayer officially opened the dedication. The stockholders survey the gathered crowd. Perhaps they share glances of satisfaction at what they see. They recognize folks from the city— their patrons, neighbors, and fellow businessmen–but that isn't the only group of people here. Rankin came through, and a lovely, eloquent article had been published four days ago. Clearly, the word had gotten out, as a number of farmers and other country dwellers from around the county had found their way here as well. Whispers of approval are circulating in the throng. The day seems successful, but the lots haven't gone up for sale yet. The men aren't sure what to expect. They are only cemetery plots, after all.

One day, the phone rang. When the voice on the other end spoke, all of the man's fleeting thoughts and curiosities became reality. Glenwood's board wanted him for the job. He never thought it was likely to happen. Caring for a cemetery is such a peculiar thing. But here he was in the position to accept a job that had always intrigued him. He was looking for work anyway, and Glenwood had found him and was staring him in the face. The opportunity was irresistible.

Before long, he and his family moved into the caretaker's house. He would take care of the finances and would open and close the place daily. That was all that he would be responsible for.

After living there a while, he decided that Glenwood had more value than most people thought. A conversation with a friend set him embarking on a new endeavor. Sure, the cemetery, whose age and terrain renders it interesting, is a great place for an afternoon walk, but he realized that there is much more there than it seems, mysteries to be uncovered. The past handful of decades had traumatized the area. The very things that had catalyzed Glenwood's development—a booming population, industry, wealth—had passed on, blight and poverty acting as their weathered headstones.

Flint succumbed to amnesia; it needed help remembering. And the man—Peter Lemelin—knew that, with its acres upon acres brimming with memorials, Glenwood was up to the task.

Once sales began there was "lively" competition for lot selection. The dreams of the stockholders had been realized, and their expectations were surpassed. The men may have congratulated one another on their accomplishment, surprised that many peoples' selections were "deferred ... to a future day" because they hadn't time to complete a system hearty enough for the demand. They had only to supervise the care of the place going forward and revel in the compliment that the positive response paid them.

As time went on, maybe they looked over the names on their roster—businessman and patrons, politicians and constituents, doctors and patients—and realized the feat that they had accomplished. Or maybe they remained partially ignorant of what they had done. Perhaps they only knew that they had completed what they set out to do—create a place of splendor and solace for the living, in honor of those who were dead. Maybe certain things can only fully be recognized when the smudge of the present is wiped off the lens.

They had created a place of paradox, a society unlike any other. People of varied occupation, income, and social class mingle there in death in a way they never would have in life. Orphans rest aside multigenerational families. Enemies are buried in proximity. But most of all, it became what they had hoped, a place of repose for the living as much as, or even more than, the dead. What was once a place of peace in a bustling city remained a place of peace in a groaning one.

Peter set out across Glenwood's grounds with a pen and paper, his silent companions. He stopped in front of monuments, gleaned names and dates, and carried his new discoveries back to the old house at the main gate. Then, much like the men that designed the place, he got to the real work. He took an idea and brought it to life. He Googled and researched and noted. He took the names of all-but-forgotten people, extracted the bones of their stories bit by bit from the dust covered past, and rearticulated them into relevant, pride-inducing narratives. He compiled and organized and collaborated until finally Peter had collected the support and information he needed to resurrect Glenwood.

A less realistic man might have ignored the people whose tombs lie in permanent shadow. He could have ignored tragedy and pain, but Peter realized something important—those stories matter too. They are a part of history that must not be forgotten. So, he collected the worst of stories alongside the best.

Near the back of the western section of Glenwood towers an elaborate monument. Atop, a figure, probably Jesus, clutches a cross—the Latin resurgam, or "I shall rise again," lies just below. At the base, the surname Newton is embossed in all capital letters, and around the cube that makes up the space between is a series of names. Yet, above this noticeable, but otherwise normal, memorial looms an apparition intangible but powerful—legend.

The turn of the 20th century was less than a decade away. An aged Judge Newton traveled east from his home in Flint on "pressing business." When he announced the trip to his friends and associates, he left his intentions vague, but a few observant people noticed his lighter demeanor and suspicious stop at a jeweler's. He returned about ten days later. He had taken a young woman named Grace, a beautiful, voluptuous brunette with dark eyes, to be his bride.

William Fenton Newton, their son, was born a couple of years later. About five and a half years after the birth, on August 31st, 1900, a shot was fired in the Newton household. Grace had been struck in the abdomen. She succumbed to the injury on September 6th, and was buried—against her explicit wishes—in Glenwood Cemetery. But here is where the fog between real life and legend grows dense.

The account told to Peter by the family paints Judge Newton as an unsavory character. The story says that someone owed Newton money, someone that couldn't pay, so in recompense Newton could marry their young daughter. He was sketched as the kind of man who had his wife, who was supposedly cheating on him with a staff member, murdered at the hands of a mysterious gunman. When questioned, Newton supposedly used his young child as his alibi.

The other portrait—the one that was smeared in the press—is of an unhappy young wife that took her own life. The coroner listed the incident as suicide, but the presence of the word "supposed" in the report seems less than definitive. Yet, the woman appears to have written a will for the occasion. She even outlined how she wanted her body to be handled—cremated and then thrown to "the four winds" by her friend and fellow prominent Flint resident, William Crapo Orrell.

There is little doubt that gossip swirled in the lives of William and Grace Newton. He was old and reserved; she was social, popular, and prone to garnering the attention of men. The day-to-day workings of their life are unclear. The only apparent thing is that their union was a tumultuous one. The complete story of her death—what actually transpired that August day—may always be a haze that hovers in Glenwood, one of many mysteries buried alongside their subjects.

Peter's dedication, much like the cemetery's, paid dividends. On his own time, he took many of the narratives and arranged them into a tour. In a span of about ninety minutes, as they walked from grave to grave, he would tell participants what made Flint great, the people that had spent their lives building it. A group of local historians were the first to tour the cemetery; their new guide offered them the narrative skeleton he'd constructed. His nerves were on edge. They were the experts, not him. But Peter pushed through, and in the end, that first sale was a success. His efforts were praised, and he was encouraged to continue on.

As always, the newspapermen were watching the proceedings, and a reporter for the *Flint Journal* followed Peter around the grounds shortly thereafter. They meandered down the paths—the same ones Peter had traversed throughout his lifetime, stopping to listen to the stories, the lives, that the stones represent. A short time later, the article outlining the reporter's experience of Peter and his work at Glenwood was put in print, and the tours gained in popularity. In 2009, the year after Peter was hired, Flint—perhaps in the most unlikely of places and in the most troubling of times—had found a source of pride again.

In 2014, due to financial struggles, management shifted to Detroit's historical ceme-tery, Elmwood, and Glenwood lost the man who had poured his passion into pulling this forgotten place out of the past and into the present. The person who cared enough about Flint and about the people whose collective stories comprise what Flint is and was is gone. The old house at the gate is now a usually empty office. The phone number belongs to Detroit. And the stories and pride unearthed are at risk for reinterment. The walking tours are no longer available.

But once a year, that element of Peter and Glenwood's intertwined past, a Me-morial Day of sorts, is celebrated during Back to the Bricks, a time when car buffs flood Flint's main street to celebrate automotive history in the heart of Vehicle City. As part of the festivities, people are invited to stroll down Glenwood's pathways, listening as costumed actors recount many of the same stories that Peter had ex-humed.

"We didn't know who we were," Peter said. Though some of his plans were left unrealized, he did what he could to change that. He tried to help the amnesiac remember her past, so she could better visualize her future.

Flint lost Peter Lemelin, but as long as Glenwood's gates swing open each morn-ing, there is always the opportunity to discover, to tread those paths just as he did again and again, to draw our own meanings from the place, to keep Flint's collec-tive memories alive.

Dubiously Flint: Remembering (and Forgetting) My Grandmother's Stories

KATIE CURNOW

T his essay is about oral history, guilt, and identity. It's an exercise in amateur archival work, genealogy, and research. Emphasis on amateur. I wrote this essay on lunch breaks and on my phone, one-handed, while I nursed my newborn son to sleep. These are not excuses; these are facts.

There are twelve, maybe thirteen, children picketing in a black and white photo I am looking at. Some hold signs with solidarity messages, "We're behind our dads 100%." There are two signs I can't quite read, but very clearly can see the words "BETTER FOOD...BETTER LIFE." My grandmother, at eleven years old, stands in the snow among the group ranging from toddlers to teenagers. Her twin sister, one child between them, is dressed in a matching outfit. Both girls are holding signs in mittenless hands. My grandmother's reads, "OUR DADS WILL WIN! Join the Union." The signpost partially covers her face and, the older I get, I'm less and less certain it's her at all.

I don't remember the first time I heard it or who told me, but for many years as a child, I knew one thing about my family and about Flint: "Your grandma was in the sit-down strike." It would be years before I could understand the importance and reality of one of the most iconic moments of my grandma's life, of Flint's history, and of the foundation of labor and work in this country.

To be honest, I'm still working on that understanding.

We were living in a small house in Burton, a Flint suburb, in the late '80s, early '90s. My grandmother, visiting from northern Michigan, had just shown me how to tap dance in our small kitchen. Well, the rudimentary steps involved in tapping. Twenty years later, I distrust my memory of this dance sequence and the terminology. Maybe it was heel-step-toe. Maybe it was ball-step-toe. Heel-ball-step? I remember having my hands on my hips, head up, a tin man of a child with a Kool-Aid mustache, while she clapped along to my stiff movements. In that same kitchen lesson, I remember her teaching me the local school fight song. I can't remember one word from it. It would have been at least forty years since she sang the song as a teenager, and she knew every word. Many things my grandmother taught me I've forgotten or misunderstood or have had to relearn: sewing, baking, appreciating Shirley Temple. As my perspective shifts and things once ignored now move into a place of importance, I've lost something greater than kitchen skills and craft ingenuity: an oral history of my family. A history interwoven with Flint and with work as we know it. Or knew it.

The lines of my family's history intersect with the infamous industries and events that shaped this city. In some ways, Flint shaped my family. The stories I've been told, about grandparents, great-grandparents, have impressed upon me certain values and points of pride whether true or not.

"Uncle Loring invented the color 'candy apple red' for Buick."

"Grandpa graduated from Kettering, but back then it was called GMI or some version of that. And it was a high school. I think it was a high school. Well, I think it was Kettering."

"They decided to strike in a secret meeting in grandma's basement."

"Here's a spread about great-grandpa in a magazine for DuPont. He came from Cornwall to work in the mines in the U.P. then made his way south to Flint."

"That's my grandma holding the picket sign."

Each year the history becomes more like myth as I no longer remember the details and my imagination fills in the plot holes of the stories. But these stories, many more truth than tale, anchor me to this city. In a place where so many have fled, I sometimes question why I want so badly to prove I belong. Like a genealogy of place, I mark moments on a tree, Flint the trunk and my family's experiences all branches. Here's my proof, my roots, these growing myths the leaves at the tops casting shadows downward.

There's something at stake for me, for my identity in that image of my grandmother. In writing this, am I trying to prove my roots in Flint? Is it the sit-down strike? Where in this world does this place and that event have more weight but here within the city limits? Who am I trying to impress? Or who am I trying to convince I belong? Is this about Flint-authenticity? Establishing that I am Flint-made? Maybe. Again, why does that matter when the state, the world seem to barely acknowledge this city and its residents. What does it mean to want to be unified with the forgotten and ignored?

As a child, I saw the picture of the children picketing in a newspaper article com-
memorating the Flint sit-down strike that someone had clipped as a keepsake. This
memory rolled around in the back of my mind like a pebble in a tumbler, becoming
increasingly refined and altered over time.

Recently, I interrogated my parents regarding the locations of a few family historic objects, the newspaper photo included, as I prepare to pass down these relics
and stories to my children and investigate my own understanding of them. "Where's
the picture of grandma? Was she in the photo? Do we know it's her for sure?" I
searched for archived issues of the newspapers online that I could access for free to
see if her name was mentioned or if she was interviewed. I struck out.

I spent a few semesters as a research assistant while attending the University
of Michigan-Flint. Though some of the role hasn't applied to life outside of grad
school, two lessons have: library archivists are helpful creatures, and the avail-
ability of digital records makes armchair research accessible to now lazy, busy
writers/workers/mothers. I tracked down the photo housed at the Walter P. Reuther
Library at Wayne State University and hoped for some verification that it is indeed
my grandmother in the photo. The archivist, helpful indeed, gave me a date for the
photo: January 10th, 1937. Eleven days after the Flint strike began.

The archivist suggested that I learn about the Women's Emergency Brigade and
about Genora Johnson Dollinger, a mother to one of the children in the photo and
an activist in her own right. I learned that Dollinger organized the children's picket
line, that she rallied support for the men striking and for their families. She was
strong, charismatic, and determined to see change happen for the better of many.
She's the kind of woman I thought I'd grow up to be.

Though the archivist helped me plot the photo on a timeline and directed me to
some important resources, there was no confirmation that my grandmother is pic-
tured among the young picketers. I would have to keep looking.

In my youth, I imagined my grandmother in the plant, sitting on dirty floors,
missing her home and unsure why she would have to be there at all. To be clear,
my grandmother was not in the sit-down strike, and until recently, I thought her
father, my great-grandfather was. There's a box in the archives of the University of

Michigan-Flint with my great-grandfather's name in it from an oral history research project conducted in the late 70s that included over 170 interviews. Box #9. He was never interviewed. I'll never know what he had to say. I found out about that box not by digging through the archives at the university, but by clicking around the digital space of the archive when researching for a college essay about ten years ago.

Google becomes a proxy for my grandma. Oral history is now clicking; it's search bars and magnifying glass icons. She died in 1995, two months after Genora Johnson Dollinger. All the questions I should have asked come twenty years too late, and I'm Googling, desperately trying to find information on my great-grandfather's role, on my great-grandmother's involvement, anything to validate these stories.

As I work through some of these leads, I realize it's not what I'm looking for, it's whom. There's a finality to the storytelling, to the myths. All it takes is one generation to forget. Then what stories will they tell? Will I tell? Why we are here. Who we once were. Who we could be. There's something to hearing our stories from the mouths of those who lived it.

I was twelve at the time of my grandmother's death, as close in age as she was when the fate of her family was in the hands of industry, when her stories would stop and my mind would need to retain the sound of her voice and the way she narrated. All memories of her are filtered through a prepubescent lens with a focus on Christmas gift inventories over our family stories.

It's possible I'm wrong, misinformed, and my family is not involved in the sit-down strike, that this was all a big family misunderstanding. Even then, I want so badly to be close to it. I want to be involved. I want to value the labor struggles of men and women before me. I want to support, not exploit, the city that slips away year by year, that degrades and crumbles like the brick streets under the weight of our vehicles, and relentless pressure from outside forces.

But I am the outside. I live in the suburbs. I see the city on the horizon as I get on the highway for my daily duty, in my rearview as I return home at night. I have the privilege to leave the city in whatever state it's in that day, to leave my anxieties at the boundaries of some real or imaginary city line. I sympathize from afar. Always too afraid to hold my own sign, I've looked to others as their arms grow weak and tired and admired their strength to show the world their words, their desires. How do I show solidarity with a city that means something to who I think I am from another zip code? How do I show gratitude for the life I live because of others? To be in the same place and roles now as my great-grandparents, to be a working mother married to a working father, hoping our best is enough, split between our realities and our ideals. I easily take for granted my home, my children, my time as mother, worker, friend. There's my grandmother with her sister picketing in the winter of 1937, her father fighting for his future and his family's, and where is her mother? What did she do as mother, worker, friend?

If that's not my grandmother in the photo, and her father was not in the plant, and her mother did not work with Genora, it still matters. It happened despite the mind's attempt to create mythology from history. Though I don't live in the city, I care about the people who have, who still do. And they deserve to tell their stories, to be remembered, for their fights and hardships to matter. We're surrounded by these stories, reminders of a strong past here in Flint, but it's easy to feel like they never happened. There's value in these Flint stories, in our relatives' narratives. I'm not the only person shaped by those here. After decades of mistakes and struggle, we, they, shouldn't have to fight this hard, carrying their own signs demanding a "better life."

What stories can we recall? What lessons will we have to relearn?

A People's Park

EMMA DAVIS

ey! What're y'all doin?" he yelled across the empty park. A pint-sized paper bag sat on the sidewalk next to his smooth-soled tan work boots.

He's directly in our pathway, I thought, as my assistant director, Mel, and I emerged from underneath the Saginaw Street bridge downtown at Riverbank Park. Forty feet ahead, a man lounged on a concrete bench built into the supporting wall of an overhead platform—a former market block stall where people had once sold goods. His flannel coat was the same worn shade as his blue jeans. An amoeba-shaped wet spot darkened the pavement a couple feet away. It wasn't the first time we, two blonde women in our twenties, were on the receiving end of an unsolicited comment at the desolate park.

"We're rehearsing for a performance. About Riverbank Park," Mel said as we neared the bench.

"Ohhh," he said, sounding unsure. "Where will it take place?"

"At the park," I said. "It's a show about the history. The audience travels around the different blocks while watching music, theater, and dance. It's based on park history and community memories."

He thought for a moment. The warm September breeze rustled the three-year-old trees rooted like litter in the grassy canal meant for water. He smiled, revealing a missing tooth on his bottom jaw.

"You know I come down here once about every two weeks. Used to come down here as a kid," he said.

Mel and I exchanged glances. Darkness was falling earlier each day and we still had more scenes to run through. Over the past year, I engaged community members with the park and its history to create a greater sense of appreciation for the blighted space. After a series of workshops the previous summer, we had begun to devise a script that integrated music, acting, dancing, and elements of people's real reactions to the park to create something that brought the audience to a deeper understanding of the space. We were used to excited or nostalgic reactions when people learned about the Riverbank Park Dance Project, but time was running out on this particular evening, and there were only a handful of rehearsals remaining before opening night.

"Well you'll have to check out the show then," I said, handing him a flyer for *Riverbank Park: A Beautiful Future*.

"Yeah, I'm 51 now," he continued. "Used to work at GM, in the factory. Wanted to be an electrician, but couldn't get that job. I got an associate's degree. You know, I could probably manage a Burger King if I wanted."

Working with a group of twenty artists the previous two months didn't leave Mel and I much time to rehearse our own roles as park tour guides. It was our job to deliver the historical information. Outside of creating the piece with the other artists twice a week, the two of us squeezed in rehearsals after work and classes, often with less than an hour before daylight disappeared. With the performance only a week away, we were going to have to maneuver out of the unexpected conversation, especially since he was sitting at the starting point for the last scene we needed to practice.

"There was just a trail, a pathway, along the river, before the park was built. I was in high school in the '80s, used to hang out here with my friends. You know, some of 'em may still be the same people," he said, chuckling, staring at the river as if re-watching an old film from memory.

I don't remember my first experience with Riverbank Park, except that it was when I arrived as an UM-Flint undergraduate student in winter 2008. Growing up an hour's drive south of Flint, the crumbling concrete park seemed unsafe compared to the tidy, small-town landscaping I was used to, where the neighbors shunned anyone with grass taller than a week's growth.

The strange park seemed to me like the rest of the city's worn and hidden spaces. I'm sure at one time it was a breathtaking attempt at uniting the city's waterfront with a public space that spanned five blocks of downtown on both sides of the Flint River. It includes a farmer's market area, waterfall walls, Grand Fountain, Archimedes' Screw Block, and an amphitheater surrounded by a canal that, when filled with water, creates an island stage on the river. Cracked vertical concrete walls give the park a labyrinthine feel and in some areas they create blind spots that may have been intended to create a romantic sense of seclusion, but now feel like spaces where someone could jump out at you from any direction. Broken glass litters the below-street-level pathways and overgrown scrub trees rise out of trash-filled canals. The nauseating smell of dry urine mingles with the odor of stale fish and mucky water. Only the peeling wooden signs naming each block give clues that it's a public park.

But I soon became more interested in the abstract features as I kept walking to and from the dance studio, just north of the park. During this same time, Flint was finally regaining businesses downtown after a thirty-year recession. A series of redevelopment efforts led to new restaurants, businesses, and a farewell to midcentury eyesores like the nineteen-story Genesee Towers, the city's tallest building (and arguably its ugliest, constructed in a high-modernist style), until it was imploded in December 2013 after a decade of vacancy. A tall chain-link fence encircled the building to keep pieces of falling concrete façade from hitting passing pedestrians and cars.

By 2012 I had moved to the city to work as a UM-Flint dance faculty member. Riverbank Park became as familiar to me as my own home a mile away. I often visited the park to hang out with friends after art walks and explore the maze left by the waterless Grand Fountain. It was unlike any park I'd ever experienced, which were often just large, grassy fields with some play equipment. Without a working water system to bring it to life, only a concrete skeleton of the park remained. But the more I went there the more I felt the spirit of the space and those who'd been there before me. I fell in love with the architecture of the park because it was a perfect space for creative movement when it was empty of water.

But my love for the park was threatened when the City of Flint received a grant award in 2012 to remove portions of the park's concrete features. This was when I first learned Lawrence and Anna Halprin's connection to the park.

Riverbank Park was designed in 1976 by the office of Lawrence Halprin and Associates based on public suggestions and the Army Corps of Engineers' flood control requirements. The park's design intended to bring together the community's idea of aesthetic and spatial beauty with Halprin's best practices in how public spaces encourage interaction. He often worked with his wife, pioneering postmodern dancer Anna Halprin, whose process-oriented approach to dance inspired Lawrence to develop the RSVP Cycles, a collaborative method that seeks transparency for diverse groups working together. Together, the Halprins worked with communities to include them in the design process by exploring and discussing public spaces and their effects on human experience over time. When opened, Riverbank Park won several architecture awards, becoming a space for the community to gather and create memories.

With a sense of urgency from the pending construction, in 2013 I took a week-long workshop from 93-year-old Anna Halprin at her Mountain Home Studio just north of San Francisco. I learned how Anna's method combined dance, visual art, and storytelling to create deeper understandings of our environments and personal experience. One day we explored the redwood forest in her backyard to ask a tree a question, and then answered by drawing, writing, and dancing a response. The results symbolized events happening in our own lives, bringing understanding and visibility to the forefront. I wanted my own community to feel a similar transformation when reflecting on Riverbank Park.

Riverbank Park was nicknamed the "people's park" when it first opened in 1979. With the early auto industry boom, Flint's wealthy industrialist forefathers planned many of the neighborhoods to have their own parkland, creating around 60 parks across the city. Riverbank Park is designed very differently, serving as both a flood control project and feast for the senses. The park spans five blocks beginning on the north side of the river at the Archimedes Screw Block, which moved water up from an old dam to a series of canals connected below the street bridges and includes a "water wall" of small waterfall-like single stream fountains shooting down a smooth concrete wall. The rest of the water would continue forward to the Grand Fountain, with an intricate series of smaller fountains and pools for residents to swim and play in.

On the south side of the river two additional blocks were built, one that originally included a kayak launch and a series of market stalls. Beyond that block was the large amphitheater that surrounded the concrete island stage, divided by a canal. The canals could only be filled when water levels hit a certain height, so an additional inflatable dam known as the Fabridam, was included at the southern end of the park to retain water and raise the river to fill the canals.

Riverbank Park was one of several projects to attract tourists and support economic development during the beginning of what would be Flint's multi-decade recession. By the late 1960s and early '70s, a declining auto industry and layoffs led to increased crime and poverty, and suburban "white flight" began to empty out much of the city. As a company town tied to the fate of the auto industry, Flint was hit hard by the oil crisis of the early '70s, and as population shrank the city made many attempts to stop the loss of residents and revenue.

The park brought new energy downtown when it first opened in 1979. The amphitheater stage was host to headliners like Dizzy Gillespie. During the initial performance of my project, one of the audience members mentioned that he was at the original opening, and country singer Rick Nelson entered the island stage by floating down the river on a boat. I've spoken with several people who shared childhood memories of playing in the Grand Fountain, going to Kids' Kapers events, meeting Mr. McFeely (the mailman from *Mr. Rogers' Neighborhood*), and attending the Flint Jazz Festival for the past thirty years.

But problems began soon after opening. A businessman, for instance, was walking along the boardwalk on the north-side Water Wall Block, and he tripped in one of the gaps in the concrete. Soon after, the gaps were covered with steel plates, also covering up the ability to connect directly with the river. There were issues with late-night partying, thefts, assaults, vagrancy, vandalism, and the park's north and south divisions on each side of the Flint River became a symbol of the city's underlying racial boundaries. The park also suffered mechanical and electrical problems, and according to the *Flint Journal*, people would try to pop the Fabridam with bullets, arrows, and knives.

The park was designed optimistically but perhaps not realistically. The canals only fill with water when the Fabridam artificially raises the river level. The canals were meant to be full of water, but because the Hamilton Dam existed at the park's northern edge, there needed to be a creative way to raise the water high enough to enter the canals. Eventually, the crumbling dam required that the river level stay low so that too much pressure wasn't put on the it, leaving the canals dry and full of trees and trash.

Perhaps most symbolic of Riverbank Park's tribulations starting in the 1980s, was the 25,000 pound, 40-foot-tall, yellow aluminum sculpture on the amphitheater stage. Created by a Buffalo, NY, artist, the modernist sculpture was intended to be a crowning jewel for the park. However, five months after installation, the sculpture fell into a canal and broke after a windstorm. It took two years before it was bolted back together and reinstalled, with steel cables added later. The artist even took out a mortgage on his house to help fund the repairs. But in 1984, the city removed the sculpture, citing safety and legal concerns, and when a buyer was unable to be found, the city decided to scrap the metal. The sculpture was replaced with a pine tree.

In 2012 the city of Flint received a grant to increase park accessibility south of the river. According to a city planning department report, the construction included removal of concrete portions in the Amphitheater and Market Stall blocks, filling in canals with dirt, a new kayak launch, and a handicapped-accessible ramp leading to the Amphitheater stage. I wanted to be happy for the changes, but I couldn't help wonder how much time remained before Riverbank Park was just another failed attempt at a brighter future, soon to be demolished and forgotten by the next generations. Or at least, that's what it can feel like here sometimes.

"There used to be this Archimedes Screw at the park," the lounging man said, sipping from the can wrapped in its beige paper blanket.

My interest sparked. He recited a line of dialogue matching what we'd imagined a character saying in our script. While I've never personally set eyes on the Archimedes Screw, I knew what it was from talking with residents and searching *Flint Journal* archives. Archimedes invented the spiral design in 200 BC to pump water out of leaky ships, and it was later used for irrigation systems, allowing cities to flourish with a direct water connection.

"Yeah, it was right next to Hamilton Dam," I said. "Haven't talked to anyone yet who knows what happened to it."

"It's an old invention designed by some Greek or Roman guy…maybe Socrates," he said.

"Or…Archimedes?" I responded with a smile.

His expression went blank for a couple seconds. Realization spread across his face as he processed the name connection and laughed it off. Mel responded with her line from the show about how the Archimedes Screw was initially installed backwards, and how the gears had to be reversed in order for it to work properly. An ominous sign that perhaps should have signaled how the park's, and Flint's, history would unfold.

Learning about the history gave me a stronger connection to the space, and I wanted more from this once-beautiful park. I wanted others to see it as I did. How, I wondered, would the community respond to Riverbank Park if I used Anna Halprin's participatory dance methods in the space designed by the office of her husband and collaborator, Lawrence? I wanted to bring the area to life and use its many secret and underused spaces to get visitors moving through the park as it was originally intended, hoping to create a connection that would inspire future visits and increase awareness to what a resource Flint had in front of its eyes.

In 2014, two years after the initial grant award, construction still hadn't started and I wondered if the city, operating under a state-appointed emergency financial manager by that time, would decide against the changes with only a year remaining to utilize the funds. That summer I developed a series of workshops that would inform the 2015 performance. Together, both parts were known as the Riverbank Park Dance Project. The four workshops gave participants a hands-on experience in the space using Anna's movement methods while discussing park history and responding through art-making. The three, multidisciplinary performances led the audience throughout the park's main blocks and were based on interactions with the space, as well as park history, poems, art, and dances created during the 2014 workshops.

During the workshops, we started at the Amphitheater and Market Stall blocks, exploring areas using Anna's scores with movements like sitting, standing, walking, and lying down. Traveling each of the four main blocks, we discussed history and current issues about the space. At the Grand Fountain everyone shared their experience of the park by drawing a picture, writing a poem, and creating movements.

Many of the drawings imagined the park's potential, with multiple shades of green grass and blue water flowing through the canals and fountains. Poems articulated challenges. One poem written from the perspective of the park said, "I am not very old, but I feel like it. I used to feel much stronger now, but I've fallen ill recently." Another poem: "The glorious plan for the space has been lost, but, it still has a purpose. It's part of the earth and as the trees shelter the walls, it continues to exist to the world, wants to be seen." For movement responses many people did "the wave" with their arms, where one arm lifts and floats back down while the other arm echoes to look like rippling water. Of the 50 people we surveyed, half had not been to the park before and every person said they would likely visit again.

The workshops identified what people thought of the park currently, but embracing memories was essential to the performance. I held two story circles, or dialogue sessions, to better understand how people have personally interacted with the park.

A story circle is a method that values the voice of each person while identifying reoccurring topics important to the whole community. I've participated in story circles for other creative projects in Flint, and enjoyed how the technique provided opportunity for residents to be involved in the creation of the performance. At our Riverbank Park story circles, people said they wanted more activities like the monthly cookout a local church group had for community members and homeless people. Women felt unsafe at the park, and people worried about the next-door neighborhood, Carriage Town, a historic area one woman said was a place she was afraid she would get robbed.

In June 2015 a chain-link fence the length of a city block surrounded the Amphitheater, and demolition began. With my fingers interlinked with the fence, my heart cracked as I watched a multi-ton wrecking ball slam against the stage bridge. The thunderous echo of concrete smashing into concrete sounded like a dumpster being dropped after emptying.

Luckily the performance worked around the closed Amphitheater Block, and even incorporated it into the performance with music and a dance in front of the fence, acknowledging the weddings and jazz festivals that happened there. Rehearsing outdoors in the middle of summer wasn't easy, with some days reaching temperatures above 90 degrees, but we were committed. Each rehearsal I prepared a score or narrative based on the information I'd been researching, and in return each artist developed their creative response, many utilizing the architecture for a connection with the space. About half of the artists had visited the park before, while the remaining had never been before rehearsals started. In the beginning, most said the idea of a performance taking place at Riverbank Park was different and unusual, but by the end everyone agreed it was a good experience that helped to change perceptions.

The performance opened the last weekend of September 2015, and attracted around 200 people. The title, *Riverbank Park: A Beautiful Future*, was inspired by a park fundraising brochure created in the mid '70s. We raised $160 and it was donated to Flint's Downtown Development Authority for future park clean ups.

Starting at the Market Stall Block, the audience traveled throughout the park on a historic tour. The site-specific show included scenes depicting a 1970s park fundraising pitch, fishing, parkour, dancers representing nature and activities like playing in the water, music from festivals over time, the construction changes, and an entire scene at the Grand Fountain that included poems and movements created by workshop participants, voicing hopes for the park's future.

During talkbacks, audience members ignited conversation about the park's past, present, and future. For those who had been there before, it brought back both painful and joyous memories. Many people agreed on what they'd like to see at the park, including several types of art, and brought up issues of safety, maintenance, and cleaning. There was a desire to see the water features working again, specifically at the Grand Fountain, and hopes that the Amphitheater changes would help bring people to the park, despite some skepticism about the city's ability to follow through with the project successfully.

"It was built with a purpose," an audience member said about Riverbank Park during the last performance talkback. "Part of the Halprin process was to incorporate movement, and you can see the necessary changes to revitalize it are still typical to witness, but the necessary changes to bring it back to life...the key to any park is to have people be able to actually participate in it. Parks don't exist in a vacuum. Without people being there, it's all for nothing."

Listening to the man's stories about the park, Mel and I saw a dark, wet stain on the concrete near his feet. We shared an awkward look with him before he broke the silence.

"You'll have to excuse the urine," he said, pointing to the squiggly spot. "My friend peed there."

By this time, I was familiar with every nostril-burning stench at the park, but this random act of urination felt personal.

"Why didn't he just go in the canal?" I asked the man, annoyed about his friend's choice to pee in our pathway.

Analyzing the tall grass in the canal four feet away, he laughed. "I agree! But he just stood up, went right there, then left."

I was used to suspiciously smelly puddles at the park, but they were usually under a bridge or secluded corner. Not just out in the open.

"You know it kind of felt like he did that in my house," he said, pointing to the spot. "I was just sitting here, having a nice time, and then my friend got up, and went, right there. And then he left without me!"

The three of us were there, stuck with the stale smell of evaporating urine. We all agreed it was a jerk thing to do. Our experiences of Riverbank Park weren't necessarily the same, but our appreciation for it was. It's a place where we've met people and made memories that shaped our lives.

We got to the point where I found an opportunity to practice my line from the performance, about leaving. We thanked him for sharing his story and said we needed to get back to rehearsing. After reminding him of the show dates, we walked up the stairs leading further into the park, away from the concrete bench. Dusk was on the horizon and Mel and I still needed to practice our last scene as tour guides. I spoke the first line:

"Maybe it's obvious Riverbank Park isn't the shiny modernist gem it used to be, but it's the people--"

"Hey!" He shouted across the empty park, the paper bag clutched in his hand. "Mind if I go pee here?"

Only if it's in the canal, I thought, as Mel and I stood frozen with mouths open. Our eyes locked and silently asked: Was there a friend? Was that his wet spot from earlier? Is this guy really going to pee in the canal right now? There's no public restroom so maybe it would be the most...courteous thing to do?

Then, he laughed.

"I'm just kidding!" he said, throwing his arms up into the air.

And we all laughed, as he turned around, walked away from us up the stairs towards Saginaw Street., and left the park.

Bathtime

CONNOR COYNE

The bath delights her.

When it's 6:45 in the evening—dark or getting darker—and we ask her, "You ready to go night-night?" Ruby toddles over toward the stairs, muttering, "bobble, Geegee." A bottle of milk. Geegee, her stuffed giraffe. She is one year old.

Her eyes light up when we carry her into the bathroom. We drop the plug and press down the plastic mat—you don't want little babies slipping and banging their heads on the hard porcelain—and fill the small room with the silver sound of falling water.

She gives us a big smile as the lukewarm bath surges up around her sides. She laughs brightly when she sees she can make waves by slapping her hands down against the water. She feels buoyed by the bubbles between her toes, the fine mist that catches in her light, pixie hair. She grabs for floating foam letters, a plastic turtle, a rubber duckie. This is one of the happiest moments of her day, and it's good that she is happy before we ask her to keep calm in the darkness, to let her brain slip into sleep, to stop moving for awhile. Bath as benediction. A sacred quietness that slips between the Flinty clatter of distant train wheels rolling. The familiar thrill of train whistles. A reminder of her baptism.

For Ruby, the bath is an immersive experience, and so she tries to dip a plastic cup in the water and take a big gulp. Little kids are immune to parental squeamish-nness. They do this all over the world, or at least anywhere little kids take baths in porcelain bathtubs. Squeamish parents cringe and say, "No, no, we don't do that. We don't drink water from the tub."

In Flint, though, our reaction is more severe. We lurch forward, our faces pale. It's like catching your toddler tottering at the top of a flight of stairs. It's like seeing a preschooler running headlong toward a busy street in pursuit of a plastic ball. You feel it, visceral in your gut, like someone sucker punched you and you want to puke. They might be making themselves sick from something much worse than suds and whatever scum has been washed away by the day's play.

My wife isn't from Flint.

I am.

Well, I grew up in the city until I was twelve, when my parents moved out to Flushing, a picturesque suburb that finally got its own coffee shop in 1997. That was the year I graduated high school. But even though I had a Flushing address, I auditioned for every play at Flint Youth Theatre and went to the Flint Central High School prom. I always considered myself a Flintstone and spent as much time as I could in the city. When I went away to college in Chicago, I always hoped to come back home. To me, Flint was a place of youthful energy and risk, frisson and connection. I was aware that I was the salmon swimming upstream, against the current of all the other people eager to leave, but I didn't care.

When I met my eventual wife a few years later, I regaled her with all the stories of my friends and their fucked-up lives. The insane intensity of life in Flint. The city had been abandoned, I said. Physically abandoned by the company that built and nurtured it, and then again by half of its people left struggling in the wake of deindustrialization. Psychically abandoned by a state and nation that had little patience for what they saw as retrograde rust, the unrealistic expectations (they thought) of a populace that expected luxury but lacked the ingenuity and the work ethic to hold onto it. Were these assumptions justified? That was one question she might ask. I would shrug. Occasionally, I might say. Usually not. What was key, though, was that this place broke everyone, and the brokenness made us like Jesus. Conscious suffering, self-aware suffering, opened us up to beatification and grace. We Flintstones cracked open like Easter eggs that offered our provisional yolks as a sacrifice to testify to the flawed construction of the world and its human institutions. Or maybe we were just Buddhas who emptied ourselves inside out so that we could move forward as that best of blank slates: an erased American chalkboard, ready to be filled with knowledge and questions, to offer hope and transcendence to the world-at-large, and to find peace for ourselves. Inner peace that existed independent of external poverty.

For my wife, practical concerns edged out my visionary rants.

I wanted to go back to the place she said that seemed to break everyone I knew (my fault for building the perception, after all, since I told her about the pedo that chased two friends through Woodcroft—the rich neighborhood—in his car, even while my friends in Civic Park and the State Streets—poor neighborhoods—saw neighbors' house light like jack-o-lanterns and burn down on a fiery autumn night)... how on earth was I going to promise my children a happy, stable childhood in this, my fucked-up home?

"I got this," I said.

I actually felt—and I'm not bullshitting here—more able to deliver that happy, stable childhood in Flint than anywhere else. See, in Flint, I knew the rules. It isn't chaos. There are rules. There are especially rules if you're 1) middle-class, 2) white, and 3) educated. And the college education supplied by my father's almost forty years at GM under UAW-earned contracts got me there. My kids would have friends here. They would live in a stable neighborhood and go to a good school. They would have educational opportunities, we'd keep an eye on them, and it wouldn't be any more difficult or risky than a life in Chicago, or New York, or New Orleans, or San Francisco. It would be safer, less risky, because I knew how Flint worked. I didn't know how those other cities worked. I didn't know their rules. I had the tools to control a child's experience of Flint. Anything else, I'd be learning from scratch.

I said this with a lot of arrogance and a fair amount of truth, but hubris always lands the punchline.

When our first daughter was born, we decided to leave Chicago and move to Flint. Because of the fallout from the 2008 housing meltdown, we could afford a house south of Court Street, just east of Downtown. When I grew up, this was one of Flint's most exclusive neighborhoods. Now, a family on a single income could land a beautiful 1930s Tudoresque house for a down payment less than that of the tiniest Chicago bungalow. We could use the money we saved to choose any school for our daughter we wanted. We were close to my parents. We were close to friends. I planted a garden in our back yard and put up a swingset and a fort. The front yard was filled with dappled sunlight that streamed through the maple leaves each summer, enough shade to cool off, and enough sun to nourish the petunias, iridescent in their violet summer glory.

It was cool.

I knew the rules.

I didn't know the rules.

The rules were bullshit.

I was thinking about classroom sizes and museums and violent crime and copper scrappers. I was thinking about street violence and friends from broken homes and arson and unemployment. Too many guns and too little supervision. These were the problems I was trying to puzzle out. Meanwhile, the city went under state receivership and started drawing water from the Flint River instead of the Great Lakes by way of Detroit. The rest is a sad story told across the world by now: the river water wasn't treated properly; it leached lead and other junk from the pipes into tap water. A lot of people drank that water. A lot of people got very sick. Government officials tried to cover up the catastrophe, leading to more sickness, more delays, more damage.

I had never banked on the water going bad.

In all my youthful exuberance, my desire to bring my girls up here, in my community, my pride, my home, I thought I had covered all of the bases, but water is fundamental, the number two necessity for humans after breathable air. A place that tries to damage you with its water is damaging in the most basic way. And so, I stayed alert each night, watching Ruby bathe, conscious that this isn't right, that this is supposed to be safe, that she would only be safe, for sure, through our unfailing vigilance.

Ruby doesn't know that the water in this city is bad. Dangerous.

Mary, her five-year-old sister, understands it in a straightforward way, like Darth Vader, like busy traffic, a risk to be avoided. She knows that she shouldn't drink the water just like she shouldn't talk to strangers in strange cars. This loss of innocence and the anonymous lies that prompted it make me sad and angry. Sometimes, it keeps me up at night, thinking of all the injury, the hurt, the real hurt, physical, mental, the loss of trust, the enormity of that loss, the immensity of betrayal, the contempt of those officials who have treated us—treated our children—like expendable animals. Lab rats. Numbers and statistics that might be converted into a political liability, and what a pain in the ass we are for that reason. I've dreamed about it more than once. What if the tests the city conducted on our household water were wrong? What if we didn't act quickly enough? What is this place going to look like in fifteen years? Who is going to be left?

Mary is a bright five-year-old. She is old enough to understand some of this. Not old enough to feel the outrage, but old enough to notice the contradiction and confusion. It's expensive, we tell her. Why can't we drink it? she asks. Well, I tell her, you can wash your hands in it, but don't drink it. Don't you drink it. Even if it's the middle of the night and you're thirsty, come and wake me up. I'll get you a glass. You're right. The world isn't right and the world isn't fair.

Some of these are conversations every father expects to have with his child, but not so soon, and certainly not about the unsafe tap water that costs you $130 each month. Not in the first state to light its darkened city streets with street lamps. Not in the U.S. state that put the world on wheels and taught it to move with speed.

Ruby isn't even two yet. She doesn't even see the confusion of contradiction. For Ruby, the confusion is much more simple: she likes to dip the plastic cup in her bath water and take a drink when she can. We freak out, lunge forward, snatch up that cup, and toss it to the floor. Ruby yells in surprise and disappointment, the loud noise, our worried faces, the brief chaos of moving hands and water spray.

She'll relax again, in a few moments, when we soothe her with a song, or give her something else to play with.

We'll relax, too, when the last of the water has finally vanished down the drain.

Contributors

Gordon Young is a journalist and author of *Teardown: Memoir of a Vanishing City*, a Michigan Notable Book for 2014. His work has appeared in the *New York Times, Politico, Washington City Paper, Slate,* and *Next City.* He is the publisher of *Flint Expatriates*, a blog for the long-lost residents of the Vehicle City. He grew up in Flint's Civic Park neighborhood and now lives in San Francisco.

Layla Meillier is a mostly lifetime Flint resident. She is a workaholic and University of Michigan-Flint student; she enjoys odd jobs and doing theatre at Flint Youth Theatre. She lives in a neighborhood rich with stray cats and crackheads with her partner, a local musician.

Jan Worth-Nelson is editor of *East Village Magazine*, retired from a twenty-six-year career as a writing teacher and college administrator at the University of Michigan-Flint. She is the author of *Night Blind*, a novel based on her experiences in the Peace Corps. An Ohio native, she has lived in Flint since 1981. Her essays, poems and stories have been published in the *Christian Science Monitor, Contemporary Michigan Poetry,* the *Los Angeles Times, Michigan Quarterly Review, Midwest Gothic,* the *MacGuffin,* the *Torrance (CA) Daily Breeze, Passages North, Fourth Genre, Witness* and elsewhere. Her thesis for her Warren Wilson College MFA was on architecture and poetry, and she remains entranced by the effects of roof beams, corners, and the light through windows on human life.

Eric Woodyard is an award-winning journalist working at *MLive.com-Flint.* Woodyard is a 2006 graduate of Flint Southwestern Academy and a 2010 graduate of Western Michigan University. He is a native of Flint and author of the book *Wasted.* He has interviewed stars such as LeBron James, Russell Simmons, J. Cole, and Steph Curry. He has one son, Ethan, and lives in Flint Township.

Teddy Robertson was raised in California, lived in Poland over four years, and has remained in the Midwest since she returned to the U.S. to complete a doctorate in Slavic Languages and Literatures at Indiana University. She arrived in Flint in 1984, and her early experience was shaped by the promise and collapse of Buick City. She has resided in three of Flint's neighborhoods—the North End, Glendale Hills, and Mott Park. She retired from UM-Flint as Associate Professor in History.

Bob Campbell was an electrician at AC Spark Plug and later a staff writer for the *Flint Journal*, the *Lexington Herald-Leader*, and the *Detroit Free Press*. He grew up in the Elm Park neighborhood on the south side of Flint.

Stephanie Carpenter is a prose writer currently living in Michigan's Upper Peninsula. Her work has appeared in *Witness, Nimrod, The Cossack Review, Crab Orchard Review*, and elsewhere. She is most often blue and blinking in agitation.

Patrick Hayes is a Michigan-based writer and communications professional. He's a former reporter and editor with the *Flint Journal* and *MLive.com* and has contributed to ESPN.com, SB Nation, the *Detroit Free Press*, *The Classical* and *SLAM Magazine*, among other publications. Visit his website at patrickhayes.net and follow him on Twitter @patrick_hayes.

Traci Currie is a Jamaican American poet who grew up on the east coast and pursued degrees in Communication Studies at the University of North Carolina Chapel Hill and Ohio University. She has been performing poetry on stage for twenty years. She presently teaches at University of Michigan-Flint in the Communication Studies Program and co-facilitates bi-weekly spoken word workshops in the juvenile detention center.

Born and raised in Flint, **Will Cronin** is a community developer currently living and working in rural Wisconsin with his wife, three kitties, and a tortoise. He hopes to return to Flint someday and put his skills to use rebuilding the only city he's ever loved.

Rev. Becky Wilson is a deacon in the United Methodist Church, living and serving in Detroit. Her experiences growing up at the corner of Begole Street and Lavender Avenue in Flint shape her views on the world, her faith, and her writing.

Andrew Morton is a playwright and community artist who is originally from the U.K., but now lives and works in Flint. He teaches theater at the University of Michigan-Flint and is the Playwright-in-Residence at the Flint Youth Theatre. His play *Bloom* was a Dorothy Webb Prize Winner at the 2013 Write Now Festival and winner of the 2013 Aurand Harris Memorial Playwriting Award, and is published by Dramatic Publishing, Inc. See more at andrewmorton.com.

Sarah Carson was born and raised in Michigan but now lives in Chicago. Her poetry and short stories have appeared in *Columbia Poetry Review, Diagram, Guernica, the Nashville Review,* and the *New Orleans Review,* among others. She is the author of four chapbooks, and two full-length collections, *Poems in Which You Die* (BatCat Press) and *Buick City* (Mayapple Press). Sometimes she blogs at Sarahamycarson.com.

Nic Custer is a Flint resident. He has contributed to eight site-specific and verbatim plays on local topics including arson, emergency managers, Riverbank Park, and the Flint Farmers' Market.

Stacie Scherman is a journalist and storyteller working in Flint. She writes for *East Village Magazine* and founded Flint Podcasting Company, which debuts its first Flint story series in 2016. She is often asked where she finds her stories, to which she replies: Stories are everywhere. You just have to be open to receive them. Facebook.com/FlintPodcasting

James O'Dea is a poet and philosopher living in Flint with his brother, their roommate, and several other animals. He pours beer for money and loves baseball and jiu jitsu. His family has been a proud part of the Flint community for over 100 years.

Born and raised during the 1980s and 1990s on the eastside of Flint, **Melissa Richardson** is currently pursuing a master's degree in English at the University of Michigan-Flint. Her most recent publications include a poem titled "Stood Up at Good Beans," published in December, 2015 in *Qua Literary Magazine,* and a slam poem titled "Dreams" that was published at the UM-Flint Annual Writer's Conference in 2008. Her writings describe her own personal experiences and interactions growing up in Flint, Michigan.

Edward McClelland was born and raised in Lansing, Michigan, and attended Michigan State University. His Rust Belt history, *Nothin' but Blue Skies,* included several chapters on Flint, covering the Sit-Down Strike, the withdrawal of General Motors, and the emergency manager era.

An eclectic with a variety of interests, **Sarah Mitchell** spent several years wandering through a miscellany of college courses and after abandoning the notion of pursuing biology—originally conceived so she could live her life working alone in a sterile lab somewhere, of course—she settled on English. She is now working towards a master's degree with the hope of taking a cue from Dr. Frankenstein and building an eloquent monster of a career writing, teaching, and dabbling in whatever other adventures present themselves along the way.

Katie Curnow is a university marketer and literary magazine advisor. She used to live in a neighborhood behind a drive-in theater in Flint. She snuck in twice but left before the movies started.

Emma Davis is a dancer, choreographer, and educator living in Flint. Her work is primarily site-specific, drawing on personal experience and historical, architectural, spatial, and socio/economical aspects of a place. Davis directed the Riverbank Park Dance Project, a community-based, site-specific performance that shared the stories and history of Flint's Riverbank Park through music, theater, and dance.

Connor Coyne is a writer. He has two published novels and a collection of short stories. His website is connorcoyne.com. He lives in the East Village (or the College Cultural Neighborhood, depending on who you ask) with his wife and two daughters.

Acknowledgements

I was talking with Thomas Henthorn, a history professor from the University of Michigan-Flint, one day about Flint's history and he used a term that I love and that I know would make many others grit their teeth, roll their eyes, or simply be confused: "the myth of Flint."

What he was talking about was the grand, accepted narrative of Flint, that it was a city with a golden age and a dramatic fall that is now—what? It gets tricky. There are several versions of the Flint myth. Depending on which you like best, the city is now either picking itself up by its bootstraps, limping on helplessly, or simply doomed. Go back further in time and you'll learn that even the golden age—one of the more accepted parts of the myth, when the booming auto industry manufactured as much happiness as it did Buicks—was not golden for everyone and the dramatic fall was ...well, yes, that sucked all around. Still, you can blame whoever you want. The greedy high brass of the auto industry; the union; Flint itself: cursed land of the economically damned. You can pick your own version of the Flint story much the way you can read a choose-your-own-adventure novel.

Throughout the editing process, this book would sometimes accidentally be referred to as *Happy Anyway: The Flint Anthology*. It is probably only people with my particularly nerdy skill set who see the definite article in that sentence ("the") and cringe a bit. This book is not *the* Flint anthology, but rather, as the cover says, *a* Flint anthology. This is not the definitive Flint book, but rather another entry into the Flint literary canon, on the same shelf with, if I may be bold enough to say, Gordon Young's *Teardown: Memoir of a Vanishing City*, Andrew Highsmith's *Demolition Means Progress*, and Ben Hamper's *Rivethead: Tales From the Assembly Line*. It is not the first, nor should it be the last, anthology about Flint.

What you've just read is a cross section of Flint's stories—and it's one that I'm incredibly proud of and one that I certainly didn't gather alone. I would like to thank all the writers who put in the time and effort to write these stories (and for putting up with my particularly nerdy and picky skill set). I would also like to thank Anne Trubek, who once had the crazy idea that Rust Belt cities had their own stories worth reading about, and started Belt Publishing along with *Belt Magazine*. Thanks also to Martha Bayne, editor-in-chief of *Belt Magazine*, who has allowed me to continue to write about Flint, and whose keen editorial eye helped polish this book as well as my own writing. Thank you Blake Thorne, who with one text message gave my love for narrative nonfiction a kick in the pants at a time when it was very needed. Thank you Marjory Raymer, Bryn Mickle, and Clark Hughes for giving me the freedom to explore this city. Thank you to my wife, Kristie, whose unending encouragement and honesty keep me going.

And lastly, thank you Flint. You are flawed and beautiful, and I love you.